HIRE
Performance:
RECRUITING A WINNING SALES TEAM

Dr. Dave Barnett

Hire Performance: Recruiting a Winning Sales Team
Copyright © 2003 The Barnett Group, Dallas, Texas. All rights reserved.

ISBN 0-9729099-0-7

This book is available for use on the understanding that it is copyright material and that no quotation from the thesis may be published without proper acknowledgment. The right of Dr. Dave Barnett to be identified as author of this work has been asserted in accordance with the Copyright, Designs and Patents Act of 1988. All rights reserved. Printed in the United States of America. Except as permitted under the United States Copyright Act of 1976, no part of this publication may be reproduced or distributed in any form or by any means, or stored in a database or retrieval system, without the prior written permission of the author. Except for the quotation of short passages for purposes of criticism, education, and review, no part of this publication may be transmitted, in any form or by any means, without prior permission of the author. All Rights Reserved.

This book is sold subject to the condition that it shall not, by way of trade or otherwise, be lent, re-sold, hired out, or otherwise circulated without the author's or publisher's prior consent in any form of binding or cover other than that in which it is published and without a similar condition including this condition being imposed on the subsequent purchaser. All Rights Reserved.

SalesMAP is a trademark of The Barnett Group, Dallas, Texas. All rights reserved.

First printing: March, 2003

10 9 8 7 6 5 4 3 2 1

Publisher Information
This book is published under the auspices of the Academy of Market Intelligence, a foundation established to the study of business intelligence, competitive intelligence, marketing intelligence, and market intelligence.

Academy of Market Intelligence publications are printed in the United States of America and available at special discounts for bulk purchases in large quantities, corporate programs, or special needs from the author. For more information, contact:

Academy of Market Intelligence (AMI)
1616 Thorntree Drive
DeSoto, Texas 75115 – 2116 USA
Email address: contact.ami@mindspring.com
Visit our website at www.mkintel.org

Cover and book design by Keith Crabtree, *www.crabtreedesign.com*

Dedicated to

Julie, Jill, Amy and Michael

Table of Contents

Chapter 1
Getting to Hire Performance 1

Chapter 2
Confronting Recruitment Reluctance 7

Chapter 3
Strategic Recruiting 17

Chapter 4
Sales Productivity 101 27

Chapter 5
The Secret Is Balance 39

Chapter 6
Teamwork Isn't Accidental 51

Chapter 7
Designing Your Compensation Plan 63

Chapter 8
Where to Look for Qualified Candidates 69

Chapter 9
How to Write a Sizzling Recruitment Ad 77

Chapter 10
Getting What You Really Need from Resumes 87

Chapter 11
The First Interview 99

Chapter 12
Using Sales Hiring Tests 109

Chapter 13
Follow-up Interviews & Behavioral Interviewing Skills 123

Chapter 14
Making the Offer 161

Chapter 15
What We've Done For Others, We Can Do For You 169

Forward

Though much about business has changed, something the legendary Red Motley said years ago is as true today as ever. "Nothing happens until somebody sells something" was Red's way of reminding one and all that salespeople are the life blood of any company. Without the customers generated by a company's sales staff, Red liked to ask, where would the money come from to write all those checks to everyone else on the payroll?

If salespeople are really as important as Red says, then it is vital that organizations find and hire good ones. Yet many (if not most) companies have losing records when it comes to recruiting sales winners. The national average for turnover among salespeople is running close to 50%. The cost of that failure – in time, energy, morale and money – is staggering.

But it doesn't have to be that way. Companies can and should do better. And they can – if they will read this book, heed its advice, and use its tested, trusted SalesMAP™ program with potential sales hires.

Experience has proven that the greatest enemy to building winning sales teams is managers hiring on the basis of their intuitive feelings about candidates. Relying on "gut feel" is not a sound management strategy. You wouldn't feel safe driving your car across a bridge designed by mystics using "positive visualization." You want the best scientific know-how when your safety is at stake. In the same way, why would you trust one of the most important activities of your business to anything less than the very best science has to offer?

Hire Performance is a recruiting system rooted in science. I have profiled thousands of salespeople using our validated sales competency assessment, The Sales Maximizer Analysis Profile™ (known popularly as SalesMAP™). Not content with guesswork or old wives' tales, SalesMAP™ has yielded a wealth of information about all kinds of selling – direct sales, inside sales, retail sales, strategic selling. Research verifies that SalesMAP™ is more than 70% accurate at identifying who will sell and who won't. This tool has proven itself time and time again to be literally worth its weight in gold to recruiters who know how costly a hiring mistake can be in their sales organization.

This book distills the knowledge gained from that research into a compact, easy-to-read volume you'll want to refer to again and again. Whether you're just getting started as a sales manager or are a veteran recruiter, you'll find *Hire Performance* a valuable resource.

This book is not a comprehensive textbook designed to answer every question you might have about sales and recruiting. Rather than filling up its pages with lots of details and anecdotal filler material, I've tried to keep this book short and to the point. Think of *Hire Performance* as a primer – an introduction to a recruiting strategy grounded in science instead of hype.

As tough as business is, it just makes sense to use whatever tools are available that can make management of a company or a department just a little bit easier and lot more profitable. This book and SalesMAP™ are such tools. They can and will help you find and hire the kind of sales successes your organization wants, needs, and deserves.

There are so many people who have helped make this book possible and to whom I am deeply indebted. Professor Jack Allday of Northwood University has spent many hours helping this project take form. His many years in sales and marketing have been a tremendous resource in helping me turn dry research into concepts that are readable and easy to understand. Keith Crabtree helped with the design and look of the book. He's a superior designer and so very talented in ways I'll never understand, but certainly appreciate. I am indebted to Gil Pitts for his help in this project and to Tom Grooms at AMI for publishing this work. I have been very fortunate to have worked with such a winning team of professionals.

Chapter 1

Getting to Hire Performance

I'm a sales prognosticator. I get paid to predict which potential salespeople will make their companies money and which will cost much more to hire than they will ever generate. Over the years, I've been getting pretty good at it.

I've been challenged by eighteen major companies to predict top-producing salespeople from a hodgepodge of reps. They made it tough on me. Every salesperson was positive, outgoing, and capable. Not a ringer in the bunch. They were all good enough in face-to-face interviews to have persuaded experienced managers to hire them. But some had succeeded. Others failed. A few teetered in the middle. Unlike their managers, I wasn't allowed to see or talk to a single one. In fact, several companies wouldn't even tell me how long the reps had been with the company. Remember Johnny Carson on the old Tonight Show? If you do, you'll know what I mean when I say I felt a little like Carnac, only it wasn't an envelope I held to my head, but a score sheet from my Sales Maximizer Analysis Profile™ (known on the street as SalesMAP™).

SalesMAP™ is a behavioral core competency profile I developed in 1997. Unlike personality tests that attempt to make inferences about behavior on the basis of what people "are," SalesMAP™ asks questions about what people actually do in selling situations. This 96-question assessment is my number one tool for making predictions about how someone will perform in a sales job.

In almost two dozen scientifically validated research studies, SalesMAP™ has proven to be 84% accurate at differentiating top producers from mediocre ones. That success rate grows to over 90% if you compare the scores of your top salespeople and people who have never been in sales.

Want to know my secret? It's not magic. It's science. And you don't have to be a rocket scientist to become a top-notch prognosticator yourself. This book contains what I've learned from my study of sales productivity and research into hiring salespeople. I've condensed three decades of sales and sales management experience into a system you can use to improve your odds at hiring top sales talent.

The Science of Sales Prognostication

The secret of successful sales prognostication is a straightforward three-step process. It's the scientific method you probably learned about in junior high school. Observe. Measure. Repeat.

Step 1: Observe

Watch salespeople in their environment. Determine what it is that differentiates successful salespeople from those who fail. Perhaps even more importantly, pay close attention to the observable behaviors and skills of top producers from the merely mediocre.

Stay away from evaluating potential on the basis of ephemeral and subjective mental states. This is very difficult to do. In a recent experiment we asked 400 recruiters what makes a successful salesperson. We cataloged over 45 different qualities, and every one of them was a subjective feeling state. Recruiters said they were looking for attributes like "perseverance," "positive attitude," "belief in what they sell," and other similar mental states. There's nothing wrong with any of these except they are not observable or measurable. What may be one rep's perseverance may be another's stubbornness. How do you know if one salesperson's attitude is more positive than another? Hire Performance is rooted in behaviors that are measurable. If you can't measure it, you can't manage it.

Ask yourself what are the specific behaviors that lead you to conclude that someone possesses perseverance? Do they make more calls than other people? Work longer hours? What are the markers of a positive mental attitude? Do they smile more? Are they more courteous? Learn to observe. Look for the actions that differentiate top performers from poor producers. Those are the verifiable success factors that spell the difference between selling success and failure in your selling environment.

Step 2: Measure
Once you think you know what the success factors are, next you must figure out how to accurately and reliably measure them. In order to compare one individual with another, you need a reliable way to gauge the presence and amount of that quality.

You may think top salespeople possess that certain elusive something you call "pizzazz." But that's just a word – a mental concept. How do you measure it? Is "pizzazz" the same in everybody? Most books on selling and recruiting like to talk about the "art of selling." Beware of any approach that portrays selling as an art, as though salespeople are born that way and selling is a mixture of luck and unexplainable chutzpah with definitions of success residing completely in the eye of the beholder. Determining the measures of observable behaviors turns art into science. Hire Performance works because it's grounded in scientific principles that allow any recruiter to repeat the success of recruiting a winning sales team.

Step 3: Repeat
In addition to being measurable, science requires that whatever success factors you're observing must be repeatable. They are not singularities in a cause and effect universe. If you say "pizzazz" makes successful sales reps, then you must statistically demonstrate that "pizzazzers" really are more successful than everybody else. After all, the broken clock is still correct twice a day. It's possible some people without pizzazz become great salespeople while other "pizzazzers" fail miserably. Science doesn't demand perfection. It does require you beat the odds of chance.

When you have a repeatable standard that works, you develop a system. You standardize the hiring process. You put everybody through the same routine. Science will continually improve itself because it is rooted in the truth of what actually is rather than in the wishes and needs of the prognosticator. If you, the prognosticator, put some people into the system but allow others to bypass the process, science dissolves into intuition.

For most of my professional life I've been observing, measuring, and creating a system that works. I've put everything I've learned about picking sales winners into this book so you can participate in and directly benefit from a recruiting system that works.

The book follows this same three-step process. In the first four chapters we'll observe the act of recruiting and the behaviors of successful salespeople. Part 2 focuses on a measurement tool that has proven itself to be very reliable, accurate and easy-to-use. Although the tool is not required for learning about sales science, you can still benefit from the insights it provides. You'll learn not only what success factors to look for, but also which popular success myths to avoid. Finally, in Part 3, you'll find a carefully planned program that you can repeat with every candidate to help you achieve excellence in your sales organization.

Tools You Can Use

If you're uncomfortable with recruiting, you're not alone. My research with sales organizations suggests as many as 60% of managers are uncomfortable with some aspect of recruiting. Approximately half of these recruitment-reluctant managers are so discouraged they are actively planning to leave their current position in search of a less demanding career.

If you know your recruiting isn't what it should or could be, don't feel guilty. This book is not intended to psychoanalyze you or try to change you. You've got enough on your plate without having to undergo remedial therapy, too. Recruiters are on the hot seat every day to produce results. In this book I'm going to share with you some tools, which, along with some important insights, will help get the recruitment monkey off your back. You may never feel like a natural-born recruiter, but that doesn't mean you can't build a solid sales organization.

Hire Performance is an approach to recruiting that is built on science and provides busy managers and entrepreneurs with field-tested tools that help build highly productive, dynamic sales organizations. You'll learn where to look for top candidates, how to write exactly the right kind of job ad, how to get at the truth hidden in a resume, and the tell-tale cues to motivating higher productivity from your reps. This system is a comprehensive program to help you find, train, and retain a great team of high performance salespeople.

Although I've tried to be thorough, this book will probably not answer every question you could ever ask about sales recruitment. Whenever you deal with people, it's impossible to perfectly predict every situation and need. If you're new to recruiting, this book can help get you up and running, or at least headed in the right direction, as quickly as possible. If you're an experienced recruiter, Hire Performance will make you even better with creative new ideas and research-based solutions to your greatest challenges.

Throughout the book, I'll be telling you more about SalesMAP™. I strongly believe that without SalesMAP™, hiring decisions are likely to be mystical and subjective. I'm not saying intuition should be entirely abandoned, but relying too heavily on your "gut feel" about a candidate greatly increases the probability of hiring the wrong person.

SalesMAP™ will make your recruiting easier and more productive. However, as good as SalesMAP™ may be, it should never be used as a substitute for your professional sense and interviewing skills. **That's the purpose of this book: to arm you with the latest best practices in the field of sales recruiting as well as refresh and reinforce your sales recruiting skills in the light of current research and the massive cultural and technological changes that are impacting the discipline of selling. You can be a "hire performer."**

How to Use This Book

Hire Performance is a "system." All the pieces work together. Each part reinforces and supports the others. Follow the system as I've designed it and you will not only recruit a better team, but you will do it with less stress and more enjoyment than you ever thought possible.

As you read this book, some subjects will interest you more than others. But you should read it all. Make notes. Keep track of your ideas and questions. Some of your questions may be answered as you read further. Those that aren't may form the basis of further study and discussion.

Like any tool, the Hire Performance system is designed to be used over and over again. Recruiters must constantly adjust to changes. As you change jobs, face new competition, encounter the ups and downs of the market, you want to revisit the material, build new skills and gain fresh insights into yourself and your career.

OK, let's get started.

Chapter 2

Confronting Recruitment Reluctance

For those charged with recruiting a winning sales team, hiring is a sales manager's most important duty. Nothing is more important than hiring – not paperwork, not analysis, not corporate politics, not motivating the troops, nothing. These aspects of management are necessary, but they are essentially meaningless if the front-line recruiter can't put together and keep together a top quality sales team.

There are as many myths about what makes a great recruiter as there are about what makes a successful salesperson. Everything I've learned about sales top performers also applies to top gun recruiters, because recruiting is selling.

Recruiting is the toughest sales job of all. Why? Because recruiters must sell salespeople. Because good salespeople can spot another good rep, the best candidates are likely to avoid working with a mediocre recruiter.

Recruiters struggle and frequently fail for the same reasons salespeople fail – they don't make enough sales. They don't add enough of what they get paid to produce to the bottom line. Why? Is it because they have lousy personalities or aren't thinking positive thoughts? You can make the answer as complicated as you want. But it comes down to this. Recruiters fail when they don't consistently do the high pay-off activities that success demands.

Mediocre recruiters, like poor performing salespeople, spend more time, energy and resources in administrative trivia than recruiting. Some get more wrapped up in administration than making calls. Others would rather hold meetings than prospect. Still others allow rearranging files to take precedence over following up leads. For many, office politics and gossip are more pleasurable pursuits than getting referrals.

This obsession with distraction and excuse making is called "Recruitment Reluctance."

Recruitment Reluctance refers to all the barriers recruiters develop to initiating contacts with potential and current clients. Customer contact is the core competency of all sales jobs, including recruitment. It's impossible to make a sale if you haven't established a connection with a customer. Sales don't mysteriously appear from heaven. Business must be developed by conscious effort. Products and services can be promoted in many ways – print, broadcast media, Internet, word-of-mouth. But the universal, irreducible, sub-atomic activity in every sales situation is the person-to-person contact. Buyers must hook up with sellers.

As a "middle man," recruiters market in two directions simultaneously.

In order to find these candidates, sales managers must develop extensive networks of people and organizations as sources of referrals and lead generation.

They must contact employers able and willing to pay for their service.

While independent recruiters and headhunters know the importance of prospecting employers, the in-house sales manager may overlook this critically important dynamic. The sales manager in a company may not call other businesses, but the she or he must always identify and learn to satisfy "internal customers," the people in the organization who depend on the recruiter doing the best possible job. Internal customers for the sales recruiter include everyone who has a stake in the business generating more profit. Top notch recruiters make lots of contacts to the people in the organization who can make a difference in what the manager earns.

Good recruiters, like great salespeople, make lots of contacts with the right people. Poor performers don't see enough candidates or promote themselves effectively within the organization. These are the individuals who suffer from Recruitment Reluctance.

Many who struggle with recruiting initially deny or repress their contact reluctant feelings with self-confident optimism. They pretend and lie to themselves. Bravado can work, but only for a while. Most businesspeople can summon up the courage to walk across hot coals once, maybe twice. But recruiting is an every day activity. Eventually, the pretending and mind games set up enormous psychological stress, which, in turn, exact a huge toll on the recruiter's energy and attitude. Recruitment Reluctance is about coping. To muddle through, managers learn to avoid what is uncomfortable, keeping themselves busy with other management activities.

Recruitment Reluctance blinds managers and recruiters to the contact dependency of their work. If you want to build a winning sales team, let's look first at you – the recruiter. If you do have Recruitment Reluctance you must identify it and confront it now.

Recruiting Performance Checklist

The Recruiting Performance Checklist will help you do a quick diagnosis of your recruiting aptitude. Please answer the questions on the following pages as honestly as you can allow yourself to be. No one will see the results but you. The more candid your answers, the more likely you will benefit from this exercise.

Recruiting Performance Checklist

Circle the answer that comes closest to describing your answer to each of the following items.

1. Within my industry, I would evaluate my current recruitment efforts to be:
   1. Far below average.
   2. Somewhat below average.
   3. About average.
   4. Somewhat above average.
   5. Far above average.

2. When I was "in sales," I considered prospecting a necessary evil.
   1. True.
   2. I was never in sales, but I would have probably not enjoyed prospecting as much as other aspects of selling.
   3. I was never in sales, so I'm not certain how I would have felt about prospecting.
   4. I was never in sales, but I believe I would have devoted a great deal of energy to prospecting.
   5. False.

3. In our sales organization, we prefer to use another term (for example, "account executive," "consultant," etc.) less offensive than "salesperson."
   1. Very true.
   2. Somewhat true.
   3. Uncertain.
   4. Somewhat false.
   5. Very false.

4. I probably worry more than most recruiters about whether my reps are going to make it in our sales organization.
   1. Very true.
   2. Somewhat true.
   3. Uncertain.
   4. Somewhat false.
   5. Very false.

5. I've been successful recruiting a certain way and I'm not likely to change it now.
   1. Very true.
   2. Somewhat true.
   3. Uncertain.
   4. Somewhat false.
   5. Very false.

6. I'm a bottom-line person who doesn't need to spend a lot of time analyzing situations. I'm an excellent judge of character and talent.
   1. Very true.
   2. Somewhat true.
   3. Uncertain.
   4. Somewhat false.
   5. Very false.

7 As a sales manager, what priority do you give to helping salespeople feel good about their career choice?
   1. Very high; one of my top priorities.
   2. Somewhat high; probably in top ten.
   3. Uncertain.
   4. Somewhat low; something to talk about once in a while.
   5. Very little, if any.

8. When recruiting, I expect salespeople to show initiative by calling me rather than me calling candidates.
    1. Very true.
    2. Somewhat true.
    3. Uncertain.
    4. Somewhat false.
    5. Very false.

9. I could do a better job at recruiting if I had been given proper training.
    1. Very true.
    2. Somewhat true.
    3. Uncertain.
    4. Somewhat false.
    5. Very false.

10. Right now, I would estimate that about _____ of my time is spent every day in administrative tasks and meetings that prevent me from talking to as many recruits as I could/should.
    1. 80% or more.
    2. Two-thirds.
    3. Uncertain.
    4. Half.
    5. A third or less.

How to Score Your Checklist

To determine your recruiting performance score, add up the numbers of your answers. If you answered every question by circling #5, your score would be 50 (5 x 10). If you circled #1 on every item, you would have the minimum score of 10.

My Score: _____

Use the following table to interpret your score.

Score	Interpretation
10-30	Chronic recruitment reluctance. Hire performance is being significantly impacted and should be addressed as soon as possible.
31-40	Acute recruitment reluctance may be dragging down your hire performance.
41-50	Congratulations! You appear to be a Hire Performer! Very little recruitment reluctance.

Special Note to Hire Performers: The fact that you have scored well on this checklist doesn't mean you won't need to finish this book. If you're like most top recruiters, you'll be looking for every way possible to improve your performance. If you scored above 40 and are feeling somewhat content with your recruiting efforts, deduct 20 points from your score, as you are obviously reluctant and looking for any excuse to do less.

Causes of Recruitment Reluctance

Nobody is *born* a recruiter. Recruiting is a skill-set that anyone can learn. Good recruiters are not identified by any single personality trait or management style. Effective team-builders aren't all glad-handing, self-confident extroverts. Outgoing social types may have instincts that drive them intuitively to do certain things that improve their recruiting efficiency, but these are behaviors anyone can learn.

Good recruiting has almost nothing to do with optimism or "drive" or positive thinking. The fact is anyone who will do two simple things can be a great recruiter.

Learn and practice a few basic behaviors and skills; and

Invest in the tools needed to become a "hire performer."

What makes a manager reluctant to recruit? There are probably many causes, but here are a few of the most common origins.

Contact Hesitation

Many recruiters suffer a common malady found among salespeople – "Contact Hesitation."

Contact Hesitation is characterized by self-imposed limits on prospecting and client contact. It's an internal psychological and behavioral problem that makes some reps and recruiters avoid their own clients. The basic problem is they don't make enough calls – and they know it! Many don't prospect at all. Like battle fatigue, the recruiter stares at the phone and shuffles prospect lists.

Questions #2 and #8 on the Checklist diagnose Contact Hesitation issues.

Contact Hesitation is an emotional handicap that afflicts veteran and novice salespeople alike. Novices endure prospecting. I remember my manager telling me as I started my property and casualty insurance business, "You'll have to do a lot of prospecting at first, but when you succeed you won't have to do that as much any more." I believed it, and when I had built a very successful agency, I stopped prospecting. However, when I stopped prospecting, the business stopped growing.

I did what a lot of novice reps do – I suffered through those hundreds of prospecting cold calls, eagerly fantasizing the day when I wouldn't have to put up with this "necessary evil." It wasn't until years later that I finally understood this experience as one of the influences that created my Contact Hesitation.

As a sales veteran, I stopped prospecting as soon as I had developed enough key accounts to maintain my "comfort zone." That's when my career started to plateau. It wasn't because I didn't believe in my product or that I wasn't motivated to succeed. I had a case of Contact Hesitation because, in my mind, prospecting was "beneath me."

The cost of Contact Hesitation in a recruiting manager is much greater to the organization than it is in an individual salesperson. The reluctant manager not only impacts his or her own career performance, but as my early sales experience showed, can also infect members of the entire sales team with pernicious attitudes and productivity-stopping behaviors.

Poor Sales Identity

Some recruiters are refugees from a sales career. They put in their time in the front lines and when the chance came to escape the daily grind of selling, they grabbed it.

Many managers won't admit it, some aren't even aware of it, but they didn't enjoy being in sales at all. They "endured." They "paid their dues" to get promoted to a "real" job. This overt or covert negative attitude toward selling leads to another source of recruitment reluctance – poor Sales Identity.

Sales managers with poor Sales Identity will not be effective recruiters of sales talent. Ambivalent feelings about selling make recruiting psychologically painful as the manager struggles to enlist others in a career he or she was happy to have escaped.

Managers with poor Sales Identity often don't like salespeople. They distrust them and uncritically accept negative stereotypes of salespeople as facts. Poor Sales Identity infects managers with an "us vs. them" mentality, assuming reps are dishonest, lazy, or not very intelligent. It's not hard to see how such cynicism could impede recruiting.

Question #3 on the Checklist identifies one telltale sign of Sales Identity issues. Recruiters with poor Sales Identity create pseudo-titles for salespeople, like "consultant," or "relationship manager." They use these alternative terms to soften what they perceive to be the negative impact of having a job in sales. When organizations sanction this pseudo-title, it sends a powerful message to managers and recruiters who are usually not even aware of the negative image of selling it communicates. Managers or recruiters may not have Sales Identity issues when they arrive at such an organization, but they are likely to develop sales prejudices soon thereafter.

Question #7 diagnoses Sales Identity concerns by asking you to rank the priority you think should be given to helping salespeople feel good about their career choice. Recruiters with poor Sales Identity invariably rank the issue higher than managers with a positive regard for a sales career.

Motivational approaches to management are another way sales organizations and recruiters become infected with poor Sales Identity. Having salespeople shout, "I love selling" at a pep rally may satisfy the anxieties of upper management, but it rarely accomplishes anything more than making reps wonder why so much energy and attention is invested in such theatrics. Maybe it's because recruitment reluctant managers don't really believe selling is an honorable career choice.

Poor Risk Management

Another cause of recruitment reluctance is poor risk management. Hiring is risky business. Accountants make lousy recruiters because they know how expensive it can be to make a hiring mistake in today's sales organization. One sales director for a Fortune 50 company says it costs the company $220,000 every time he hires a sales dud.

"Some mistakes I can undo or cover up," he said, "but my butt's on the line if I hire the wrong person."

Whether you're a hiring rookie or veteran, it's easy to feel intimidated by the need to manage the risk of a bad sales hire. If pressure doesn't arise from inside you, you may feel extreme pressure from elsewhere in the organization to get it right.

Problems occur when recruiters try to *over-manage* the risk. They become cautious in the extreme. Obsessive worry is the signature behavior of poor risk management (see Question #4). Risk-averse recruiters drive up hiring costs by over-analyzing and unnecessarily lengthening the time it takes to bring a new hire into the company.

Some recruiters fail because they *under-manage* the risk of hiring and training new salespeople. Too little concern for risk management makes recruiters image-obsessed, impulsive, impatient with details, and convinced they are intuitive judges of character and talent (see Question #6). These vain, self-glorifying managers look good, sound good, and will often impress top management with their bravado and daring. But they are toxic to most sales organizations. Inconsistent and unpredictable, dysfunctional managers devalue training and prefer to rely on non-skill-based competencies like charm and glibness. When recruiters under-manage risks, they create distrust, reduce productivity, and increase turnover.

Lack of Training

Another cause of recruitment reluctance is a lack of training (see Question #9). Poor recruiters pick up some ideas here and there from their own hiring experiences or from the war stories of other recruiters.

The field of selling has undergone tremendous changes, especially in response to the growth of the Internet and the explosion of high-tech sales organizations spawned by the information revolution.

The "old hands" may not be getting the job done because they don't, won't, or can't understand and appreciate the changes brought about by the plugged-in generation. If you answered Question #5 as true you may be in this category.

The high-dollar, high-tech sale is a completely different kind of selling from the direct sales of a generation ago and is changing the paradigm of what makes a successful rep. Today the stereotype of the backslapping, jovial joke-teller is as dead as the typewriter. Salespeople today are far more likely to be cerebral and technical in their approach. Sales cycles are longer and more complex than in the past. It used to be high-tech recruiters could work within their own industries and environments. Today, every industry is being impacted by the emerging global economy. Salespeople have to know more and work faster and smarter than ever before.

Young buyers are less susceptible to appeals to emotion than their parents. They demand information and are less likely to make purchases based on hype or out of any loyalty to a product.

Products are available today through many more distribution channels than merely the direct salesperson. If a customer doesn't like the way the automobile salesperson tried to pressure him into a sale, he can now go online and buy a car.

So, it's vitally important that mangers keep current with recruiting best practices. The changing landscape of sales marketing requires that recruiters be better informed than ever before. That's the value of Hire Performance. Consider it your textbook for proven sales recruiting technologies. Approach these chapters with an open, inquiring mind. Some subjects will be familiar and easy to grasp. Others will require more time.

Conclusion

Recruiting not only is selling, it is perhaps the most difficult type of sale there is. For the same reason a river never rises higher than its source, managers and employers who are reluctant to recruit can never put together a winning sales team. Identify any areas of recruitment reluctance and address them – now!

Chapter 3

Strategic Recruiting

You've probably seen that test that begins with the instruction – "Read through all the questions on this test before attempting to answer the problems" – and then there's a long list of complicated mathematical equations instructing you to add this and divide by that, etc. etc. etc. The kicker comes at the very end. The last item on the page instructs you to only complete the first problem and ignore the rest.

If you're impatient, these tests will catch you every time. You see a problem and start trying to solve it before assessing the whole situation. Patience is not always seen as a virtue in today's fast-paced business environment, but if you want to succeed, you must plan for success.

Recruiting a winning sales team doesn't happen accidentally. It requires strategic thinking and planning. "Strategic" describes a long-term, big picture perspective. Strategic recruiting implies more than a few gimmicky "How To's." You need to know the "Who To's" and "Why's."

Strategic recruiting helps you avoid the three worst mistakes recruiters make.

The Three Worst Mistakes Recruiters Make

Recruiter mistake #1 – rush to recruit. The worst mistake recruiters make is to ignore the need for strategic planning and just barge ahead with the task, trusting in luck, and improvising a quick solution. It's easy to do. Busy managers can certainly justify that they don't have the time or resources to dedicate to deliberation. So, they race on, hoping for the best.

It's hard to resist the pressure to hurry up and fill a position. Your top producer suddenly resigns. Your boss or hiring authority is pushing hard for more recruits. You're losing market share to your competitor. Situations like this add pressure to the already stress-filled assignment of recruiting talented sales professionals.

But small mistakes at the beginning often have catastrophic consequences later on. In the same way that a rocket firing a fraction of a second late can cause it to miss its target by a large margin, a small mistake at the outset of your recruitment efforts can cost you thousands of dollars and hours of grief downrange.

The best thing you can do as you begin the task of recruiting a winning sales team is slow down. Think about what you're doing and how you want to do it. Plan for course corrections, controls and contingencies. If you discipline yourself to go a little slower here at the beginning, you'll make fewer mistakes later. And the mistakes you do make will be less catastrophic. Strategic planning means less backtracking which ultimately allows you to go faster.

When you get in a hurry to hire, it distorts your perspective. You're not thorough. You'll be more tempted to take short cuts. You may not want to take a hard look at negative information, particularly if you've already invested a couple of interviews with a candidate. You may rationalize a bad hire as the most cost-effective strategy, but soon you're back at square one, looking for a replacement. Only now you've got to regain what you lost in hiring the wrong person.

Japanese businesspeople spend an average of 150 hours interviewing a potential job candidate. Everyone gets in on the act – from the CEO to front-line managers. In the US, it's rare for a manager to spend more than a couple of hours interviewing.

But time pressures aren't the only reason managers rush the hiring process. Many recruiters never define the attributes, skills, experiences, and key competencies necessary to the position they are trying to fill.

Recruiter mistake #2 – cloning. If you don't define a strategy, you are very likely to end up making recruitment big mistake #2 – hiring people who are just like you.

Janet was promoted to regional sales manager because of her success in the field. Her boss told her the company expected her to clone herself.

"Find people like you," the VP of Sales told her. "Find us five more 'Janets.'"

Janet believed she could spot the right candidate intuitively. She made herself the recruitment template.

This is a huge mistake. Your kids, your significant other, or your dog can think you're the benchmark of greatness in their universe, but that won't cut it in business. Hiring personality clones inserts an invisible bias into your selection process. When you use yourself as a model, ego gets in the way and undermines your ability to objectively evaluate the right person for the job.

Some call hiring people like themselves "the mirroring effect." It's a prescription for productivity problems and high turnover.

Organizations thrive when *different* social styles and personality types interact. Salespeople and their managers have preferred ways of getting things done. These preferences, when taken together, form ***styles***. Salespeople develop a selling style. Recruiters develop a recruiting style based on their preferences and habits. Diversity of styles on a team promotes creativity and productivity. Strengths in one individual help compensate for another's deficiencies. When people cooperate and complement each other's efforts, teamwork galvanizes and improves the bottom line as well. The more styles you build into your sales team, the more likely you are to intersect a broader cross section of customer styles and needs, and consequently sell more. Homogeneity is good for milk, bad for sales organizations.

When managers attempt to clone themselves, they undermine team synergy.

Do you know your behavioral style? How do you instinctively react to problems and opportunities? How do you prefer to communicate? Are you naturally more task-oriented or relationship-oriented? How do you like to be treated by salespeople when you buy something? All of these and many, many more details of daily life define your behavioral style, which we'll discuss later.

Until you understand your own preferences and sales predispositions, you don't really know if you can or should trust your gut instincts when hiring salespeople. Blindly following your instincts could be catastrophic to your recruitment efforts. You need objective feedback. That's why the first person who needs to be evaluated in the strategic process of recruiting a winning sales team is you, the recruiter.

We strongly recommend that you complete our SalesMAP™ Selling Skills assessment as soon as possible. If you take your time and don't try to manipulate or second-guess the test, you will gain valuable insights into your style.

If you don't want to take the assessment, you should talk with another recruiter who knows you well and ask him or her for some objective feedback. If you are on good terms with your supervisor, you could get some valuable feedback about your style from that source as well.

What you're looking for are some insights into yourself that will provide clues to improving not only your recruiting, but your overall professional development as well.

Recruiter mistake #3 – ignoring the cost of failure. Without a recruitment strategy, managers are blind to the true costs of a bad hire. I call this short-sighted condition "flop myopia."

Do you know what a hiring mistake costs? If you suffer from flop myopia, the cure begins with calculating the actual dollars and cents lost in a bad hiring decision. This involves looking at three outlays.

First, add up all the "**hard**" costs of your hiring process. Here are just a few examples:
- The price of running ads in the local paper;

- The cost of printing brochures, fliers and other recruitment pieces (don't forget the costs of developing these items as well);

- Running credit checks or department of motor vehicle reports (this step can save recruiters a lot of grief later on);

- Expenses for travel, meals, or renting facilities when necessary;

- The value of your time in preparation as well as the actual interview process (Too many entrepreneurs undervalue their time. It's probably the most precious commodity you lose in hiring a poor performer.);

- Contractor or employee set up costs (drawing up the contract, entering worker information into the payroll system or updating computer programs, complying with local, state, federal regulations, etc.).

Second, add to your hard costs **all training costs**. Most companies are spending more today on training than ever before. The days are long gone when all you needed to enlist a top performer was a yarn of "unlimited opportunity," a presentation book, some order forms, and a hearty "go get 'em, Tiger." Not only is the marketplace changing, but also the country's public education system is not turning out the quality of work force that existed even a decade ago. Training is critical in a workplace where many high school graduates can barely read. Sales recruiters tell me they cannot assume that job candidates have been raised with basic values of honesty, hard work, and courtesy.

Training costs include:
- The cost of training materials (like this book, workshops or materials you develop yourself);
- The cost of samples;
- Presentation books and other sales aids;
- Expenses for travel, meals, or renting training facilities;
- The value of the trainer's time.

Finally, add in your "lost opportunity" costs. Hiring a flop deprives you of income you might have realized if you had recruited a top performer. Here's the formula to figure lost opportunity costs.

1. Calculate the income of your top producer, or better yet, your competitor's top producer.

2. Subtract the average income generated by your bad hire.

3. Multiply that figure by the number of bad hires.

4. Depending on your business, you may also have to calculate into your lost opportunity costs the value of lost customers and reduced good will. Word gets around. You know you're your competitors are having trouble. If you get a reputation for high turnover or low morale, you compound lost opportunity costs by making it even more difficult to attract top quality candidates.

Flop myopia can be very expensive. Knowing the real value of a bad hire can provide you with a benchmark against which to evaluate the effectiveness of any tool or tactic you incorporate into your strategic recruiting plan. What is the cost of an assessment or a background check as compared to the cost of a bad hire? Is it a reasonable investment?

Strategic recruiting helps avoid these costly errors. The boss may only be concerned about filling a certain number of employment slots every month, but professional recruiters know more is required in order to produce a winning sales team. For one thing recruiting must be personally satisfying as well as profitable. Recruiters need to define for themselves, if no one else, why their work is important and whom it helps. Money alone is not enough of a motivating force to sustain the top gun recruiter. The reason so many recruiters become burned out and cynical, discouraged and disillusioned is because they have not developed a personal recruiting strategy that incorporates personal values into their daily work product. Cut off from spiritual purpose, work becomes drudgery.

Your Recruiting Mission Statement

Your Recruiting Mission Statement is a declaration of how and why you recruit. It's your philosophy of recruiting – the fusion of values, beliefs, and assumptions that emerge from your unique experiences. It summarizes what you do, how you want to accomplish your goal, and perhaps the purpose for getting up and facing another day of calling, interviewing, and selling your opportunity.

Your Recruiting Mission Statement should help you do a better job of recruiting. Here's how.

Your Mission Statement should provide guidelines and benchmarks for dealing with your clients, customers and suppliers. It ought to guide your thinking and acting in ambiguous situations and reduce tensions if conflict erupts. For example, if providing quality exceptional service really is your mission, you might be less inclined to argue with customers than to approach disagreements in a spirit of collaborative problem solving. Keeping your core values and goals front and center prevents short-term situations from derailing your long-term aspirations.

Your Recruiting Mission Statement can reveal inconsistent or conflicting attitudes within you that can negatively impact recruiting. For example, you may be driven to succeed in your career, but you may also carry around inside you a need to be liked and accepted by everyone you meet. These incompatible forces pull you in opposite directions. So, to avoid potential conflict you do nothing, and recruiting suffers.

Your Recruiting Mission Statement can make it easier for you to develop hiring strategies that maximize your strengths and minimize your weaknesses. If you value carefulness and believe it's important to avoid taking unnecessary risks, your approach to hiring will look very different from that of the manager who relies more heavily on intuition and the power of first impressions. Without examining your assumptions about people and work, your recruiting could fit you as badly as a size 10 shoe on size 13 foot.

Your Recruiting Mission Statement should provide stability in uncertain times. The unexpected always happens. Good people quit. Products change. Your competitor lowers price. Personnel changes and market shifts aren't nearly as likely to knock you off balance if you've identified your philosophy and keep the big picture constantly in front of you. Your recruitment philosophy can keep you focused on what is really important and provide important clues to help you identify what is productive and what is wasteful; what is important and what is merely interesting; what is urgent and what is necessary; what moves you closer to your target and what is ultimately distracting and destructive of your goals.

The Hire Performance Philosophy of Recruiting

I'll go first. I want to be up-front with you about my presumptions about recruiting. You don't have to agree with my viewpoint entirely to use the Hire Performance system effectively. But I thought it only fair that I share with you some of my basic beliefs and values before asking you to identify yours.

Selling is first and always a people business. People come first. People can make doing business lousy or great.

Recruitment and hiring are human activities that can never be replaced with machines or tests because the most important thing about an individual (character, work ethic, integrity, motivation) can only be discerned by another human being who possesses these same attributes.

Therefore, our mission is to seek and select candidates on the basis of personal qualifications first and professional experience and skills second. Skills can be taught; character cannot. Experience comes easily. Integrity is the hard part.

Figure 1

My wife says it's a little too wordy for needlepoint.

I have yet to discover the one-size-fits-all Recruiting Mission Statement. I am strongly service-motivated – putting people ahead of just about everything else. That's not necessarily "right" or admirable or even profitable. But it is what I believe and will definitely influence my recommendations for your recruiting.

Your viewpoint could be completely different. Probably is. I expect some statements might begin; "I come first. I'm interested in getting results for me." Still another manager might candidly admit, "I want something simple, uncomplicated, and reliable that will make me look good to my boss." Fine. Whatever it is, put it out there. Take a look at it. Evaluate it. Does it work to sustain you in tough times? Is it powerful enough to motivate you to get you out of your comfort zone?

This book will teach you a lot about examining candidate behaviors. But at some point you, the recruiter, must be convinced there's more to a candidate than what you see on the surface. You must be a judge of character. You need to feel like you can trust the person you hire. Yes, you hire people primarily to do something. But you cannot separate what someone does from the core values of that individual and what he or she is.

One of the hard lessons has been the repudiation of the political myth popular in the early 90's that the personal character of a presidential candidate doesn't count. Now, many wonder how the electorate could have been so addle-brained. That's what happens when a society or a manager loses the big picture.

Most recruiters and managers today make the mistake of hiring for skills and then training for work values and team ethic. But it's always easier and far less expensive to hire people who are honest, hard-working, and socially out-going, and then teach them how to sell your product than it is teaching people experienced in your business how to smile, how to get along with people, and that it's wrong to steal.

Conclusion

Hire Performance is a strategic recruiting system, designed to provide long-term perspective as well as near-term methodologies. In this chapter I've tried to identify my Recruiting Mission Statement in hopes that, if you haven't already done so, you will define your own recruiting philosophy. Your Recruiting Mission Statement should contain what you believe about people and recruiting as well as lay out why what you do is important to you and those who pay for your service. Yes, it may slow you down a little now to organize your thoughts and define your strategy. But in the long run, you'll go faster and ultimately get the jump on your competition.

Chapter 4

Sales Productivity 101

Your job as a sales recruiter is to know whether the person sitting across the desk from you can make money for you or your employer. Put simply, you get paid to filter through the BS and bravado to uncover the essentials that contribute to sales success. Recruiting assumes you know what makes someone a great salesperson and what makes someone a mediocre salesperson.

In this chapter, I'll expand on some ideas introduced in Chapter 1, laying out what I know from my research into sales productivity. Hire Performance is anchored in a scientific, research-driven perspective, not the typical sales motivational hype.

Selling as Art or Science

Judging from the covers of most books on successful selling, you'd think it had something to do with mysticism and religion. Go to any bookstore or search an online catalog for books on "sales" or "selling." Invariably, you'll find one or more of these buzzwords emblazoned on the cover:
- "secrets"
- "power" or "powerful"
- "dynamic"
- "new"
- "faith" or "believe"
- "bible"

Hype just seems to ooze from the glossy covers of most sales and self-help books. At some point you must decide whether selling is an art or a science.

One of the great tragedies in modern sales recruitment is the pervasive idea that character and work ethic can best be perceived mystically and subjectively. The philosophy of this book will probably differ from most sales stuff you read, especially if you spend a lot of time and money on motivational material. Sales gurus focus on the *art* of selling. They write bestsellers and speak to large crowds about esoteric, mystic matters like "positive visualization," "enthusiasm," "magic words," and "success secrets." Sounds like something out of a cult indoctrination manual, doesn't it?

Motivational gurus get rich persuading gullible and frequently desperate managers and their reps that selling is essentially mind over matter. If you think positively, look good, feel good, and believe unwaveringly in your product, you can't help but succeed beyond your wildest dreams. Like most new age cults, folks who trade on "the art of selling" teach that success is the by-product of intuitive, spontaneous, innate abilities and quasi-spiritual attitudes. The best part for sales gurus, though, is that you can't disprove any of it because they trade in qualities that can't be measured. How do you define "drive," let alone measure it? Can we agree on what "motivation" is? Is one person's "enthusiasm" another salesperson's phoniness? Where does ego drive stop and hubris begin?

Please don't get me wrong. I'm certainly not saying you shouldn't believe in your products or that it's disingenuous to be enthusiastic or to have a positive mental attitude. These attributes can be helpful, but they are not predictive and they certainly aren't determinative. If you get up in the morning and you don't feel enthusiastic, that doesn't predispose you to having a bad day.

Motivational definitions of success are vague and beyond accountability. What's worse, they create a horrible addiction.

Joe Recruiter is feeling out of sorts. He believes what the top guns have told him – that you can't succeed unless you're motivated. Joe sees an ad in a sales magazine for a motivational tape: "Dynamic Success Secrets of the Unstoppable Recruiter, only $9.95."

Joe orders the tape and listens to it on his way to the office. He laughs at the jokes, almost cries at the ending. The speaker is very entertaining and uplifting. Joe feels better. He's inspired. He even uses one of the jokes in an interview. Joe gets through the day.

Next day, however, Joe has lost that magic feeling. He rewinds the tape, but the second time he listens, the message just doesn't have quite the impact it had yesterday. He plays it again and again. After a while, those "dynamic secrets" begin to sound incredibly dull and stupid. So, what does Joe figure he needs? Yep – another tape!

He calls his supplier who tells Joe the $9.95 tape was only the first in a series. Joe learns if he wants the full treatment he needs the whole package of five audiocassettes for $89.95. Joe hands over the money. He's so relieved when he rediscovers that same magic feeling he felt when he first heard the message. He paid ten times as much to get the same effect, but he's feeling good again. Two weeks later he's looking for another high and his supplier has just what he needs.

Motivational solutions can be terribly addicting. Addicts are people who need more and more of something in order to achieve the same results. Joe's hooked. The motivational industry takes in over $35 billion dollars a year feeding the cravings of success junkies like Joe.

If you're used to motivational answers, I want you to know this book is different. You probably won't get any warm fuzzy feelings here because it doesn't deliver a lot of rousing pep talks on ephemeral nonsense like "the art of selling." This program grows out of scientific research.

The **science of selling** shows no evidence of any link between personality and production; between enthusiasm and entrepreneurial ability; between positive mental attitude and income. That doesn't mean you should hire introverted, non-enthusiastic pessimists. But you must examine more than the emotions a salesperson can muster up for an interview. If you're going to recruit a winning sales team, you must know what science says will truly predict outstanding sales performance.

Which would you trust more? Driving your car across a bridge designed by an engineer or a bridge designed by a new-age mystic? I don't know about you, but I'm much more likely to trust my safety to a design based on physics than a bridge built by positive visualization. It's the same with building your business or your career. Objective, scientific information will probably be more trustworthy than subjective, gut-level feelings, and they'll probably cost less, too.

What Science Says

The best predictor of sales performance is past behavior, not the emotions projected by the salesperson. Enthusiasm is not necessarily an insight into a candidate's character. The way to validate a selection philosophy is to examine behaviors. My Recruiting Mission Statement (see Chapter 3) says start with someone who is first of all honest and hard working. Learn how to ask the right kind of questions that reveal these essential qualifications without relying entirely on intuitions or emotions or the personality of the potential rep.

That's not to say that personality is unimportant. It's just not predictable. Like it or not, recruiting is about making predictions. In these pages I want to share with you what I've learned about behavior as it relates to sales performance, putting a validated, repeatable method on your side to help you even the odds a little.

Forget about the art of selling. If you're going to recruit a winning sales team, you need an *objective, repeatable* formula for talking about and measuring sales productivity. I don't even like using the word "success" because success is a subjective term, not a scientific one. Success can't be measured. One rep's success is another rep's failure. If you want to build a winning sales team you must have objective criteria. If you can't measure it, you can't manage it and you certainly can't reproduce it. The ability to know exactly what you're looking for and consistently make good decisions based on those criteria is the key ingredient to picking top talent.

There's been precious little scientific inquiry into the science of selling. Many scientists who publish books and articles about selling write about salesmanship the way a eunuch might write about sex – hypothetically and theoretically. I once worked for a sales research organization where the principle researchers hated selling and openly confessed to being terrified of their own clients. But they didn't hesitate to pass out advice on how to improve sales performance.

One sales bestseller that claims to be "research-based" says the best predictor of top sales talent is … (drum roll please) … the ability to ask good questions. Of course, probing has always been an important sales skill. But questioning skills are at best only a second-rate predictor of sales ability. Consider this simple question: **what does asking a question presume?**

Right – the rep has to get in front of someone in order to ask the question in the first place. The ability ask good questions is meaningless if the salesperson doesn't have someone to talk to.

Good selling requires many skills and behaviors, each of which has made some guru a ton of money from frustrated sales managers who still can't get their reps to see more people.

The Power of Contact-Ability

The brain is vastly complex. Imagine the immense job of coordinating the muscles and mental activity necessary to do something so simple as turning on your computer. Don't forget the involuntary activity of monitoring your breathing, blood pressure, sense of balance, etc. And yet, this complex system depends on one tiny synapse buried deep in the most primitive part of your brain. As you probably learned in freshman science, a synapse is the microscopic gap between two nerve endings. Like a spark plug, the electrical energy must jump the gap to send the impulse along the rest of the network. Billions of dendrites and axons in the brain are functioning at full-tilt to keep you aware, awake, and upright. Yet if this single, solitary connection isn't made, it's all for nothing. I'm talking about the synapse that tells your heart to take the next beat.

Selling is much more complicated than turning on a computer. Some researchers believe selling may be the highest order of all human behavior in complexity. But like the synapse analogy, this complex network of interconnected behaviors shuts down if one single, objective, measurable connection doesn't happen: the salesperson must initiate contact with prospective customers and current clients. I call this Contact-Ability. Without Contact-Ability, the sales process never begins. What does personality, birth order, education, presentation skills, or even sales experience matter if a salesperson can't or won't initiate contacts?

This synapse in the sales process has many different names. Some call it prospecting; others refer to it as cold calling or relationship building, or account penetration. Whatever you call it, it's the heartbeat of sales.

The real secret to spotting sales talent is the ability to take an individual's Contact-Ability pulse. If it's strong, our research says the candidate is 84% more likely to be a potential top sales talent than a rep with an irregular or non-existent desire to contact current or potential customers.

The reps that sell the most are those who interact with the most people. They sell more because they see or talk to more prospects. Veteran recruiters and sales managers know that selling, especially direct sales, is a numbers game. The more people a rep contacts, the more likely one is to find a prospect that is interested and ready to purchase your product or service.

"But doesn't the *quality* of contacts mean just as much as the quantity?" one HR VP asked me after a workshop. I think the bluntness of my answer shocked her.

"No."

"Well, I think you're completely wrong about that!" she blurted (obviously, she had not read the book about asking great questions).

"Tell me this," I asked, "how can you really qualify a prospect until you contact him or her?"

"He's absolutely right," interrupted the VP of Sales who stood nearby. "Every minute one of my reps spends pondering the quality of a contact is a minute of excuse-making and lost opportunity. Our top producers consistently are the people who make the most calls."

Contact-Ability is the key factor in predicting successful salespeople. The reps with the fewest barriers to prospecting and customer contact will invariably sell more. This truth is self-evident to anybody that has been in the trenches of frontline sales.

Now, that brings us to another important question. What makes one person possess more of this Contact-Ability than someone else? How do you get it? Can it be trained? What should sales managers and recruiters look for in a candidate? What are the telltale signs of good or poor Contact-Ability? Is there any way of knowing *before* you hire whether Joe or Sally SalesRep will make more calls than excuses?

To answer these questions, there is an assessment designed specifically to detect and measure the basic ingredients of Contact-Ability. The Sales Maximizer Analysis Profile™ (known on the street as SalesMAP™) asks 96 sales-specific questions about initiating contacts with prospects and clients. Armed with production data, SalesMAP™ can identify and statistically validate the variables that differentiate highly productive reps.

The reps that sell the most and see the most people are characterized by five behaviors. Hire Performance demands an ability to spot these attributes in anyone who aspires to join your sales team.

Five Benchmarks of Super Sales Productivity

These are The Big Five – five benchmarks of top producers that make or break sales productivity. Throughout this book, you'll get tips in how to see these hidden productivity factors as you look at resumes and interview your candidates. But for now, let's identify The Big Five. Learn these well.

Benchmark #1 – Energy

Energy is the "can-do" of Contact-Ability. Without enough physical stamina, reps run out of steam and are prone to quit making calls. For low Energy salespeople, prospecting becomes tedious and draining. The more energy reps have, the more contacts they are capable of making.

Top producers consistently bring higher levels of energy to their career than do poor producers. In our cross-industry studies, top guns average 30% more Career Energy (as measured by the SalesMAP™ Career Energy scale) than mediocre performers. High-energy individuals are more likely to have regular exercise programs, sleep better at night, refrain from drug use (including alcohol and tobacco), and maintain an appropriate body weight. High Energy producers are more likely to manage stress well and to maintain a balance in all aspects of their personal lifestyles: rest, play, family, community service, and business.

Outside sales seems to require more stamina than inside sales. Too much Energy can cause a telephone rep to become restless and frustrated. You'll often see phone reps pacing back and forth as they talk to customers, burning up excess energy. However, in both direct and inside sales, individuals need above-average amounts of physical stamina to be at their best.

Organizations have a huge impact on the amount of energy sales reps bring to their daily tasks. Too many sales meetings create a sedentary, less energetic sales team. Unrealistic performance quotas also erode stamina. One of the biggest energy drains in organizations is restructuring and downsizing. Reorganization drains energy by increasing stress levels and directing energy away from the primary task of selling to coping with the organizational resistance to change.

Benchmark #2 – Goal Focus

Highly productive reps invest their available energy in high pay-off activities. They do not allow themselves to become distracted by outside interests or pressures. They know the priorities that contribute to both personal and team success and they pursue these first, above everything else.

Goal Focus is the ability of a salesperson to work comfortably with quotas and sales ratios. High performers invariably have daily performance goals. They know exactly how many calls they need to make every day. Poor performers are less likely to know their sales ratios or to work them consistently. They prefer a more subjective, feeling-oriented evaluation of performance.

Suzy never did well on tests in school. She knew the material, but she always tensed up when she had to answer questions. Today Suzy's in sales and she gets quite uptight just thinking about her new daily quota of 50 phone calls a day. Suzy gets bored easily and finds it difficult to screen out distractions when phone time rolls around. In fact, she invites interruptions, welcoming coworkers into her cubicle to chat about the latest movie or most recent difficult customer.

Suzy suffers from poor Goal Focus. She may have Attention Deficit Disorder. She may suffer from performance anxiety. The reasons for the behavior really aren't important. It's the outcome we're concerned about. Even if we knew the origins of Suzy's goal averseness, we probably couldn't afford to change it. She's not going to produce as long as she resists setting goals by which she can be evaluated and her progress measured.

Salespeople with poor Goal Focus develop subjective, feeling-oriented measurements of success. When her manager asked about Suzy's failure to reach her 50 call quota, she replied that it's more important for employees to feel appreciated and respected than to be reduced to an impersonal phone dialing statistic.

Organizations undermine the Goal Focus of sales reps by refusing to provide sales ratios and by substituting performance measures other than contacts as the gauge of productivity. Managers with poor Goal Focus minimize the importance of contacts in favor of other performance measures. Some celebrate efficiency while others look for teamwork or policy compliance. By taking the focus off sales and putting it onto these ancillary, support activities, the organization creates and sustains barriers to this critical benchmark for sales productivity.

Highly productive salespeople not only set goals, but also are energized by them on a daily basis. Sales slackers are distracted by their never-ending quest for short cuts around quotas and a need to be busy with everything except sales.

Benchmark #3 – Sales Identity

Jackie decided to accept a sales job after an injury cut short his career in professional baseball. He was bitter and felt he deserved better than selling aluminum siding. Jackie hated prospecting, found door-to-door cold calling demeaning. He did what a lot of reps in a Sales Identity crisis do. He got addicted to motivational tapes. From his days in sports, Jackie knew how important it was to have the right mental attitude before going into the big game. So, he spent more and more time psyching himself up before making calls. He was spending more time coping with his sales identity than making sales, however. Eventually Jackie quit and got a "real job" as a personnel manager.

Organizations create Sales Identity crises for their reps in lots of ways, but one in particular that will poison the well of sales productivity.

Lucy thought she was responding to an ad for entry-level salespeople. She got the job. But on her first day of training, she is told, "Look, we don't call ourselves salespeople here."

"I didn't know what to think," Lucy said. "Are they going to ask me to do something unethical? What's wrong with selling that we have to be ashamed of what we do?"

One of the most effective ways to undermine long-term productivity is deflect the identity of the salesperson by turning him or her into an "account executive," "territory manager," "relationship manager" or any other title deemed by management less "offensive" than salesperson.

Top sellers love being in sales and wouldn't do anything else. Reps who don't, won't or can't take responsibility for their career choice to be in sales are highly unlikely to break out of the ranks of mediocrity.

Benchmark #4 – Sales Initiative

Among the five benchmarks, this is the single most important factor in predicting "contact-ability." After thousands of administrations of the validated SalesMAP™ profile, it is documented that top producers score more than twice as high on the Sales Initiative scale than poor performers.

Sales Initiative is a bigger problem for veteran salespeople, although some rookies may bring to their new career some unexamined bias against certain kinds of customers and contacts. A pharmaceutical rep may not even be aware of his or her discomfort contacting doctors – people perceived to be socially or intellectually superior. Other salespeople may have heard the horror stories of friends and family members burned in some multi-level marketing scheme and decide to put personal contacts off-limits to prospecting.

Novices usually respond well to training that identifies these attitudes, gets them out of the rep's personal blind spot and into the open where they can be demystified. Learning some basic skills is usually enough to overcome the neophyte's hesitation to prospect. But the old-timers are a different story. Veteran salespeople have sold to a specific clientele using a specific method for many years. Their Sales Initiative falls off as they learn to cherry-pick the best accounts. They stop prospecting like they used to when they were building their business, relying on a highly developed network of referrals. Veteran salespeople are more likely to justify their slowed Sales Initiative as appropriate to their market based on years of successful selling.

Sales Initiative is not merely the sociability or aggressiveness of a salesperson. Sales Initiative is the drive to make sales calls rather than to make excuses. Salespeople with low Contact-Ability have low Sales Initiative. Poor Sales Initiative shows up in a hesitation to prospect. In veteran salespeople, it manifests itself in poor account penetration. Reps make one sale to a client rather than getting more and more of that customer's business.

Poor Sales Initiative is a learned negative response habit to a sales contact opportunity. It is a reflex reaction. People don't consciously decide to avoid their own customers; in fact, many poor producers aren't even aware of their hesitation to prospect or develop all existing contacts available to them.

SalesMAP™ measures six specific contact technologies around which salespeople seem prone to develop avoidance patterns. Some label these patterns call reluctance. We prefer the term Contact Hesitation. Contact Hesitation festers around these contact technologies; telephone prospecting, canvassing (door-to-door cold calling), networking, asking for referrals, social intimidation (contacting up-market clientele) and making group presentations. The most critical contact technologies will vary from company to company, industry to industry, situation to situation.

Successful salespeople do not hesitate to use all available and appropriate methods of contact initiation. Poor performers have hang-ups about making sales calls that have turned into habits that pilfer their productivity by undermining their Sales Initiative.

Benchmark #5 – Balanced Selling Style

The fifth characteristic of top-producing salespeople is that their approach to customers and opportunities is not dominated by one behavioral style. Because they aren't locked into a single set of responses or preferences, great reps don't sell in merely one way. They adapt and change their sales approach depending on the customer's unique buying style.

A "style" is the collection of behaviors and preferences people develop around repetitive activities. Over time, consumers pick up a "buying style." Some buyers want to weigh all the facts before making a decision. Others are impatient and like to make impulsive purchases on the spur of the moment, relying more on feelings and intuition than fact. Still others need to be persuaded or will only buy from someone they deeply trust.

Every salesperson brings his or her buying preferences to the act of selling. It's the background against which they approach sales. Without training, most reps think their way of buying and selling, their style, is the "right" way. People with intuitive, impulsive styles become frustrated with the delaying tactics of those with a fact-gathering style. Relationally oriented salespeople have a difficult time with bottom-line shoppers who appear to the rapport-building rep as cold and aloof.

Top producing salespeople sell more because they can adapt their style to the needs of all buyers and not merely those with whom they share compatible behaviors.

You need to understand buying and selling styles in order to recruit and motivate a winning sales team. In the next chapter, you will learn a simple, but accurate model of behavior that will form the foundation for evaluating the strengths and challenges of candidates. Learn it well and you will be amply rewarded as you attempt to identify, recruit, and motivate potentially top performing salespeople.

Conclusion

Sales productivity is the result of five major factors. You will only build a winning sales team if you find people with Energy, Goal Focus, a strong Sales Identity, Sales Initiative, and a balanced Selling Style. They're out there. You can find them. The rest of this book tells you how.

Chapter 5

The Secret Is Balance

Recruiters get paid to predict performance. It is absolutely impossible for you to recruit a winning sales team if you don't understand something about human behavior. So, why do people do what they do? What will you look for if you want to forecast whether an individual is going to be a superstar or a flop? Beyond that, how will you motivate the top producer to make sure he or she stays on your team and doesn't wander off to join your competitor?

Hire Performance is different from other programs. Because it's behavior-based, I've developed a model for understanding and predicting human behavior. That model will be prominent throughout this book. It's certainly not a perfect paradigm. People are complex and often behave in unexpected, even counter-productive, ways. But every manager and recruiter, every business professional charged with helping people be more productive, needs a framework for comprehending why people do what they do.

I call my behavioral model "**Five Need Theory.**" I've tried to come up with a cleverer name. I've arranged and re-arranged acronyms in hopes of making the model easier to remember, but I keep coming back to Five Needs, because I believe it's more important that the model be correct than clever.

Put simply – **five basic needs drive career behavior**. There may be ten needs or ten thousand. But in my research I have isolated five that clearly impact productivity on the job. These five needs are *safety, control, approval, attention, and information*.

This perspective is based on the pioneering work of Abraham Maslow. Maslow said behavior is hierarchical – that is, higher-level behaviors must build on more basic-level skills. You crawl first, then walk, and finally run. That's a hierarchy. At the bottom of Maslow's hierarchy of behavior are basic survival needs. His basic theory isn't hard to understand. If you don't know where your next meal is coming from, you're not likely to care if your wardrobe is out of style. If you don't feel safe, you're going to have a tough time developing relationships or staying focused on company goals.

Five-Need theory is hierarchical. Success at one level requires mastery at the previous level. At the top of his hierarchy, Maslow referred to his highest behavior drive as "self-actualization." For our purposes, the top of the pyramid is summarized as simply "Career Needs" (see Figure 2). The Career Need of the salesperson is simple – to make sales. The Career Need of the recruiter is to deliver candidates who can maximize profit. Career Needs can only be achieved when the five Life-Needs are satisfied. Career Needs are undermined when an individual needs and values something further down the hierarchy more than they value or need what they get paid to produce (results).

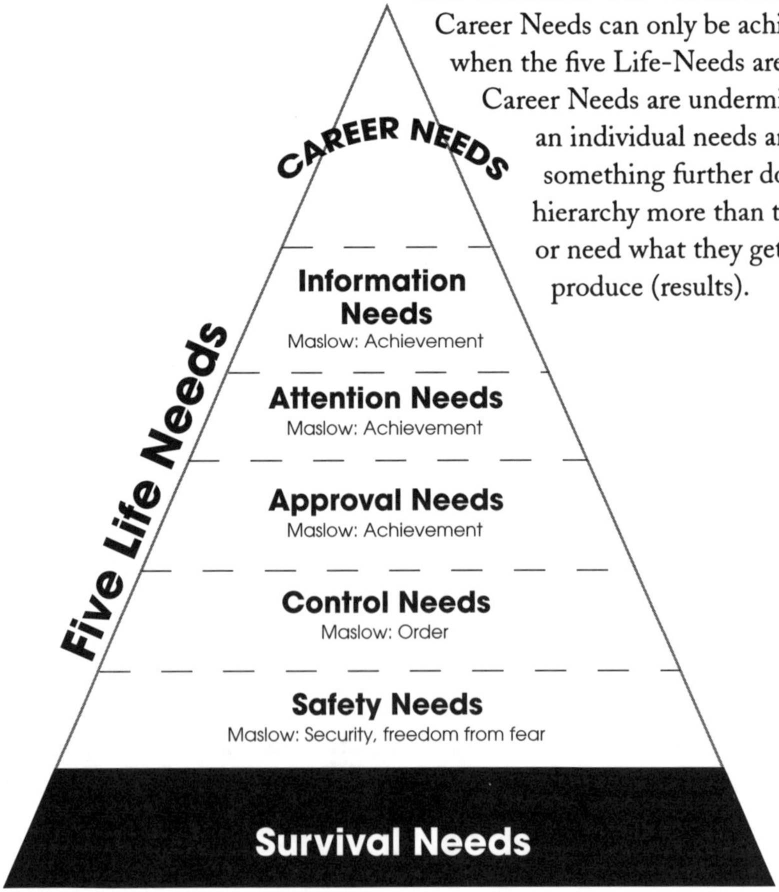

CAREER NEEDS

Information Needs
Maslow: Achievement

Attention Needs
Maslow: Achievement

Approval Needs
Maslow: Achievement

Control Needs
Maslow: Order

Safety Needs
Maslow: Security, freedom from fear

Survival Needs

Five Life Needs

Figure 2

Five Life-Needs Determine a Selling Style

Everything we do is to satisfy some desire, drive or appetite of which we may or may not be aware. So much of our daily activity is shaped by habits we hardly notice. Which shoe do you put on first? How do you respond when people say hello? Why does a person who isn't hungry snack while watching TV? Many behaviors become automatic. With repetition, we don't even think about why we behave a certain way. It becomes part of who we are. These habits strongly influence how we make decisions, particularly how we like to buy. Some people always have to think it over while others are impulse buyers. When an individual becomes a salesperson or a recruiter, those habits and preferences become one's selling style or recruiting style. Habits satisfy basic needs.

I have been able to identify five Life-Needs that are universal (they exist in everybody regardless of culture) and innate (they are in-born and not learned). Referring back to Figure 2, each Life-Need corresponds to a need described by Maslow. What Maslow called "freedom from fear," I term the *Safety* Life-Need. Reps must experience some degree of security and stability in order to be productive. Sales suffer if reps don't know from one day to the next if they will have a job.

Maslow's need for order parallels the *Control* Life-Need. Closing a sale is impossible without exerting some control.

What Maslow referred to as the need for belonging and love is the Approval Life-Need. The *Approval* Life-Need is necessary for the salesperson to accurately and appropriately empathize with customers.

Maslow's Esteem and reputation needs are similar to the *Attention* Life-Need. The Attention Life-Need helps a salesperson be socially outgoing and give good presentations. Maslow's achievement need is our *Information* Life-Need. Problem solving and analysis requires a fully functioning Information Life-Need.

Years of research into sales behavior show that top-producing salespeople have all these Life-Needs *in balance*. That is, the most productive reps aren't more analytical or more relational or more dominant. They are all of these things. One Life-Need doesn't dominate the person's behavior. Balanced Life-Needs enable the salesperson to be successful because their energy and attention are not distracted by their own personal Life-Needs.

When Life-Needs get out of balance, they produce predictable behavioral patterns. We refer to these patterns as *styles*. Buying styles and selling styles are created and sustained by the balance or imbalance of Life-Needs.

I do not know why Life-Needs become unbalanced. It could be caused by something from the individual's past, like the influence of parents, or unresolved issues from adolescence. I wouldn't be surprised to learn that our predispositions may all come down to genetics or brain chemistry. *Why* people give preference to one or more of the Life-Needs may be interesting, but usually it's not relevant to the task of recruiting. ***There is no evidence to suggest understanding the origins of these behaviors helps change them.*** Even if EEOC regulations permitted it, as a recruiter, you don't have the time or resources to invest in psychoanalyzing candidates or members of your sales team.

A balanced Life-Need means there's neither too much nor too little influence on behavior exerted by a particular Life-Need. But let a Life-Need get out of balance and the impact on buying and selling styles is profound. So, each Life-Need has three possible conditions:

1. **Balanced** (the Life-Need is satisfied and not distracting the individual from attaining his or her Career Needs);

2. **Need-Avoidant** (the Life-Need is too low and not exerting enough influence);

3. **Need-Absorbing** (the Life-Need is too high and over-influencing behavior).

Each Life-Need can be associated with a style. We'll examine the patterns of behaviors generated when someone is driven too much, too little, or "just right" by Life-Needs.

Let's assume, since we're dealing with a career-oriented program, that basic survival needs are not an issue with candidates applying for a sales job. Let's look at each Life-Need.

1. The Need for Safety

Low Safety Need	Balanced Safety Need	High Safety Need
• Reckless	Risk manager	• Risk-averse
• Not careful	Prudent	• Worries
• Thrives on change		• Needs predictability
• Risk taker	Careful	• Risk sensitive

Table 1

Selling requires accepting and taking some degree of social risk. Every contact initiated with a potential customer carries with it the risk of being rejected or treated rudely. Individuals with an exaggerated Safety Life-Need may easily feel overwhelmed in social situations. They are sensitive to every possible threat in social and business situations. They worry about all the things that can go wrong. Risk-averse salespeople often never get beyond the fear of rejection in their prospecting. Productivity suffers if salespeople aren't comfortable talking to people they don't know well and persuading them to buy something. When the Safety Life-Need is too strong, it destroys sales productivity because worried reps don't prospect. They handle stress poorly. Risk-averse salespeople get sick more than reps with more balanced stability needs.

But too little of this Safety Life-Need can be just as much of a problem as too much. Reps with a Safety-Avoidant style take unnecessary risks. They may not be careful to do due diligence. An under-developed Safety Need can hinder productivity and cause salespeople to lose sales, especially if Safety-Avoidant salespeople are selling to prospects with a high Safety Life-Need.

Of all the Life-Needs, productivity suffers most when the Safety Life-Need is not balanced. Why? It's at the bottom of the hierarchy because it's the foundation upon which all other Life-Needs build. Risk-averse reps are three times more likely to be poor producers in the organization than are salespeople with balanced Safety Life-Needs. Interestingly, risk takers with low Safety Life-Needs are not as negatively affected. But the degree to which the Safety Life-Need impacts sales depends on the type of product, service, or clientele of the sales environment. For example, salespeople who sell to accountants should have a slightly higher than average Safety Life-Need because accountants get paid to worry for their clients and probably have high Safety Life-Needs themselves.

Their worry style matches that of the people to whom they sell.

2. The Need for Control

Low Control Need	Balanced Control Need	High Control Need The Commander
• Deferring • Prefers to let others control the relationship • Dependent • Behaviors similar to high Approval Need	Decisive Takes control of the sales process Easily handles objections Self-directed	• Opinionated and critical • Not a team player • May be intimidating • Oppositional

Table 2

There are two ways individuals who feel insecure in their environment attempt to compensate for their high Safety Life-Need. One way is to become a control freak. Have you ever known people who attempted to minimize uncertainty by trying to control everything and everyone around them? If you have, you know how paranoid they may become. The second way risk-averse individuals cope with their anxiety is to over-prepare and make extensive back-up plans for every contingency. This is the Information Life-Need to which I'll return. But let's look at how the Control Life-Need impacts sales productivity.

A sale is a relationship. A sale is an opportunity to show-off both problem solving and communication skills, but ultimately selling must become a relationship with a profit motive. Money must change hands. Top performers know they have to close the sale. At some point in the conversation, show and tell ceases, rapport-building ends, problem solving and product knowledge take a back seat as the salesperson steps into a position of control and makes something happen. Selling is an assertive act of will. Those who do it best have a balanced Control Life-Need. They are comfortable with authority and know how to influence people to accomplish the goals of the team.

The Commander style is characterized by behaviors driven by an over-active Control Life-Need. The Commander becomes argumentative and can intimidate team members and customers alike. Someone who tries to over-control the sales process is often impatient with social niceties. The Commander wants to get to the bottom line quickly and will try to close a sale many times.

Commanders aren't merely individuals. Entire companies may be dominated by the values and behaviors of a certain selling style. In a Commander sales culture, reps would be trained to not accept "no" for an answer. If the customer doesn't move quickly enough to a decision, the Commander may issue the client an ultimatum or even question the customer's integrity or ability.

People with a high need for control are often attracted to sales because they are results-driven individuals who are at their best when making decisions. But in the Commander selling style, customer care takes a back seat to winning. Extremely competitive, Commanders may alienate customers who prefer a more relational approach to the sale.

At the other end of the Control spectrum are reps who don't take enough control of the sales process. They defer to clients. Control-deficient salespeople let the customer tell them when they are ready to buy. Since most customers don't do this, Control-avoidant salespeople make fewer sales. In many ways, their behaviors mimic those of the Empathizer, to whom we turn next.

3. The Need for Approval

Low Approval Need	Balanced Approval Need	High Approval Need The Empathizer
• Oppositional • Doesn't care what others think • Behaviors similar to Commander	Relationally sensitive Good rapport builder Active Listener Services the sale	• Accommodating • Fears being rejected by client • Won't close sales • Indecisive

Table 3

Most sales are built upon the ability of the salesperson to build rapport with people. Salespeople must have some degree of relational sensitivity. Very few sales are made unless the customer respects or likes the salesperson. Top-producing reps know how to be comfortable with the give-and-take of conversation. They listen well. Successful salespeople must also possess "accurate empathy" – the innate ability to sense where they are in a relationship at any given point. Does the customer like me? Accept me? Trust me? In other words, are we ready to do business? Top producers have a balanced Approval Life-Need (see Table 3).

Empathizers are salespeople in whom the Approval Life-Need has gotten out of balance to the high side. Empathizers are overly accommodating. They are uncomfortable closing sales or asking for referrals because they fear losing the approval of the prospect or client. Like a bottomless pit, they absorb all the approval in the room and still cry out for more. They do well at rapport building, but never seem to get beyond visiting to doing business. Studies show Empathizers give away more samples than other selling styles. They use gifts to win approval. Conflict-avoidant and indecisive, Empathizers are reluctant to express an opinion without first sampling the opinions of others in the group. They typically excel at customer service. It's not unusual for an out-of-balance Approval Need to drive salespeople to take the side of their customers against their own companies.

The Empathizer style is very similar to the control-avoidant rep. Their external behaviors will look very much alike. Both are relationally dependent and hesitate to close sales. However, the motivation behind the counter-productive behavior is completely different. One is seeking approval while the other is trying to avoid control.

Individuals with strong Approval needs make lousy salespeople. After risk-averse reps, Empathizers are the second worst productivity performers on sales teams.

Let's look at the other end of the Approval Life-Need. If the Approval Need is too low, salespeople don't care what others think about them and may be impatient and utterly uncaring about the relational aspects of the sale. Although on the surface it looks a lot like the Commander style, the avoidance of Approval is a far more serious condition that generates a selling style called the Oppositional.

Oppositionals can sometimes be quite productive with customers, especially very high-level decision makers who appreciate their bluntness and straightforward approach. The problems are more likely to arise with their managers and co-workers who don't understand the Oppositional need to confront and provoke almost anybody who gets in their path. The Approval-avoidant salesperson is often opinionated and seems to carry a grudge. They will intentionally provoke or intimidate others to make their point. They are not good team players. On the plus side, they are extremely loyal. Once they prove to themselves that a manager or coworker can be trusted, they will do almost anything to protect that relationship. They are as generous with those they trust as they are cheeky with those they don't.

4. The Need for Attention

Low Attention Need	Balanced Attention Need	High Attention Need The Performer
• Behind-the-scenes • Shy • Tries to hide within the organization • Behaviors similar to an Analyzer	Makes positive first impression Good presentation skills Makes work fun and enjoyable	• Impulsive • Image conscious • Talks more than listens • Self-confident

Table 4

Selling often requires a lot of "show and tell." Presentation skills are a definite asset to top producers. A balanced Attention Need enables salespeople to be comfortable in social settings. They make conversation interesting and enjoyable. They are excellent communicators, both verbally and non-verbally. This is the Performer – someone who thinks well on his or her feet, likes to be noticed, and is able to project his or her personality with ease.

If this core need becomes unbalanced, sales productivity may suffer if reps are driven to absorb every bit of attention in the environment. They focus on themselves to such a degree they don't listen to others. They are impulsive, loud, and invest more energy in how they look than how they perform. The out of balance Performer plays the role of a successful salesperson, but is usually more talk than substance. Pretenders can make a presentation entertaining, but will appear to more analytical buyers as superficial and less than sincere.

If the Attention Need is unbalanced to the other extreme, salespeople may come off as too shy or overly self-conscious. These are the salespeople who hesitate to promote themselves and are more comfortable working behind the scenes in a supportive role rather than out front where the visibility may intimidate them. Top performers are self-confident, but not vain and certainly not wallflowers.

6. The Need for Information

Low Information Need	Balanced Information Need	High Information Need The Analyzer
• Intuitive • Impatient with details • Expects quick fixes to problems	Good planner Problem solver Excels at product knowledge	• Perfectionist • Workaholic • Nitpicker • Never feels adequately prepared

Table 5

Selling is a give-and-take process. Once the relationship is formed, successful selling requires an ability to qualify prospects, ask intelligent questions, solve problems, and answer objections. Good salespeople know what they are selling and how it will meet the customer's need. These behaviors are driven by analytical skills acquired and practiced by salespeople with a balanced Information Life-Need.

When the Information Life-Need exerts more influence on behavior than other Life-Needs, productivity suffers from the individual's quest for perfectionism. The sales cycle is slowed by the "paralysis of analysis," as salespeople never feel adequately prepared for their calls. Perfectionists may do quite well at some types of selling, such as high-tech sales. Of all the selling styles, the out-of-balance Information Life-Need exerts the least effect on sales productivity. But for most direct sales, analyzing is only part of the sales process.

At the other extreme, some reps can't be bothered with too much information. They sell by the KISS motto – "Keep it short and simple." Downplaying analysis, they prefer intuitive decision-making. They act very much like the Performer. Both are impatient with details.

The Maximizer

Every salesperson knows a sale moves through various stages, called a sales process. A sales process is a sequence of behaviors, all of which require a balance of the five Life-Needs. Prospecting requires a balanced Stability Need. Rapport building demands the empathy of a balanced Approval Need. Presentation is done best by someone with a balanced Attention Need. And Closing involves a balanced Control Need. The individual with balanced Life-Needs moves from one stage to the next. Unbalanced Life-Needs subvert the sales process by either shortchanging or amplifying one stage in favor of another.

As a recruiter, you're looking for someone who is a good planner (Analyzer) AND considerate (Empathizer) AND self-controlled (Commander) AND confident (Performer).

These individuals with all Life-Needs in balance are "Maximizers." They sell more because they are better able to adapt their own behavior to match the relational, communication, analytical, and power sensitivities of differing buying styles. They may also be more successful because they work well with the diversity of styles that make up every sales team. About 15% of professional salespeople fit this high production category.

Recruiters, too, are more effective when they can adapt their recruiting behaviors to match the traits and preferences of the kind of salespeople they are trying to attract.

Hire Performance depends on your ability to spot Maximizers and to know how to satisfy individual Life-Needs to bring unbalanced reps back into a state of behavioral equilibrium.

There is so much more that could be said about these selling styles, but let's leave theory behind for a time to re-focus on the practical needs of recruiting a winning sales team.

Conclusion

In this chapter, I identified five needs that are universal (everybody's got 'em) and innate (you're born with 'em). Research proves that top producers possess all five Life-Needs (Safety, Control, Approval, Attention, and Information) in balance. Too much or too little of each can undermine productivity in predictable ways.

Chapter 6

Teamwork Isn't Accidental

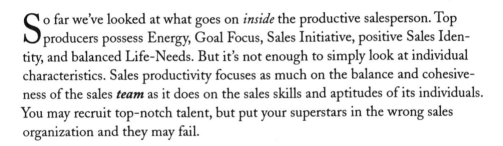

So far we've looked at what goes on *inside* the productive salesperson. Top producers possess Energy, Goal Focus, Sales Initiative, positive Sales Identity, and balanced Life-Needs. But it's not enough to simply look at individual characteristics. Sales productivity focuses as much on the balance and cohesiveness of the sales *team* as it does on the sales skills and aptitudes of its individuals. You may recruit top-notch talent, but put your superstars in the wrong sales organization and they may fail.

In addition to providing a model for understanding individual behavior, Life-Needs also provide dynamic insights into teamwork. The styles that drive reps to behave with clients in certain predictable ways also shape their approach to team behavior.

Teamwork in the Sales Environment

Teamwork is a frequently overlooked aspect of selling. Indeed, the American cultural stereotype of a salesperson is that of the competitive, solitary road warrior. Most people perceive selling to be essentially an act of one-on-one persuasion. Words like "self-starter" and "able to work unsupervised" appear continually in sales recruitment ads. About one third of sales reps say they were attracted to a sales career because they could control their own time and not have to depend on the performance of others. Sales organizations exploit individual competitiveness with contests and other incentives to provide momentary productivity boosts.

While contests may motivate some, they can discourage productivity in many other salespeople. Analyzers will carefully weigh the odds of winning with the value of the prize and may or may not participate. Empathizers use contests to build relationships with others in the organization. I've seen approval-oriented reps give away leads to front-runners and become cheerleaders for other salespeople. Empathizers care more about cooperating than winning.

Teamwork performs five critical functions in the sales organization.

Success modeling

Where do new recruits learn how to succeed or fail in their new job? Not from company-sponsored new employee orientation classes, that's for sure. New recruits watch and talk with veterans in the organization to learn the informal norms, acceptable short cuts, and performance standards. The team sanctions and perpetuates the real measures of success in the organization.

Personal motivation

Where do reps having trouble go first for counsel and motivation? Not to management. They confide in each other. Struggling new recruits confide in trusted peers. The team more than management sets performance expectations. Salespeople compare their activity to others on the team. Performance is shaped more by team expectations than decrees from the home office.

Management relationships

Even if a sales rep works alone in a territory, one's attitude and assumptions about teamwork influence the kind of relationship built with management. Great managers build strong teams. They inspire loyalty and motivate performance. How? The best managers are coaches of sales talent and not merely bureaucratic babysitters. Effective coaching assumes that both salesperson and manager value teamwork.

Strategic selling

High value sales, which take months, if not years, to close, demand teamwork. Reps must partner with multiple decision-makers and learn to rely on internal champions to move a sale through the often-complex maze of bureaucratic hurdles. Consultative selling requires getting on the customer's team.

Customer service

Attitudes toward teamwork in salespeople help shape their approach to customer service. "Lone Ranger" reps seldom follow up the sale with service. Handling complaints, asking for referrals, digging for incremental sales – this kind of productivity correlates highly with one's ability to function on a team.

Using Styles to Predict Teamwork

If you are going to recruit a winning team, it's important to know teamwork isn't accidental. Success as a team is the same as for the individual. It is the by-product of balanced behavioral styles.

Figure 3 will help you better understand the relationship between Life-Needs and the behavioral styles they generate. Balance is symbolized by the behaviors inside the inner circle. Let's use the Commander and the need for control as an example. When balanced, the Commander is controlled and persistent – admirable traits in a salesperson. As the need for control becomes more unbalanced, the rep becomes assertive, dominant, and perhaps even forceful and intimidating.

Each Life-Need in the quadrant acts in a similar way. When behaviors are closer to a balanced state (in the center of the graph), the rep is more likely to be productive. The further from the center, the more influence exerted by that Life-Need to undermine productivity.

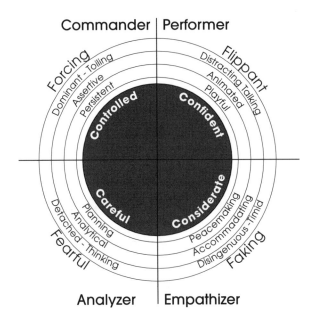

Figure 3 – Complementary Styles & The Life-Needs Balance Grid

Compatible Styles Build Winning Teams

Some selling styles complement each other. They are synergistic. The strengths of one compensate for weaknesses in the other. When you put these styles together, it can strengthen your sales team. Teamwork is maximized when personal styles complement each other.

Using the balance grid, the styles adjacent to each other are compatible. Let's look at these in closer detail.

Commanders and Analyzers

John is very analytical. He never makes snap decisions because he likes to take his time and study all his options. Decisions become difficult for John when one option isn't the clear winner over another. When John gets stuck he relies on Roberta. Roberta doesn't agonize over decisions. She may ask one or two bottom-line questions and then she'll decide the matter. John admires Roberta because she has an uncanny ability to know what's important and make good decisions.

Roberta has a strong need for control which, over time, has developed into the habits and instincts of the Commander – someone comfortable with making decisions. Commanders and Analyzers work well together. Their styles, though different, are highly compatible. Commanders like to make decisions but are often impatient with gathering details. Analyzers like to work on the fact-finding and agonize over decisions. The strengths of one compensate for the weaknesses of the other. Commanders and Analyzers are synergistic. Their styles are complementary.

Performers and Empathizers

Betty is a flashy, loud-talking sales rep who insists on being the life of the party. She tells off-color stories and teases her coworkers. Lawrence envies Betty's outgoing style, but he is also concerned about how others might feel about Betty's flamboyant ways. He laughs at Betty's jokes because if he doesn't, Betty is likely to mock him as a "prude" in front of the rest of the team, and Lawrence couldn't endure that. Lawrence knows all the office gossip. He's learned that the boss is deeply religious and is getting annoyed at Betty's coarse language. Lawrence quietly takes Betty aside at the sales meeting to relate what he's heard. "I don't want you to think I have a problem with it," he tells Betty, "but I thought you should know."

Betty's boisterous behavior is typical of Performers. The need for attention drives them to be noticed. If there isn't a crowd around, they'll make one. Lawrence is an Empathizer. He is relationally sensitive and very conflict-avoidant. Performers and Empathizers are complementary styles. Performers need an appreciative audience, someone to laugh at their jokes and admire them (or at least pretend to). Behind the Performer's back, two Empathizers might confide in each other that they think the Performer is an immature showoff, but their Approval Life-Need keeps Empathizers smiling, not wanting to offend. Empathizers have a bad habit of engaging in gossip. They use chitchat to bond with other feeling-oriented people. Performers provide them with lots of opportunities for quiet conversations around the water cooler.

Commanders and Performers

These styles are technically complementary, but they actually don't *complement* as much as they tolerate each other.

Roberta the Commander has an idea about implementing a new policy, but she's not sure how others on her team will receive it. She doesn't want to be viewed as uncertain or hesitant in front of the other salespeople, so she calls on Betty the Performer. During their conversation, Roberta skillfully maneuvers the conversation so that Betty thinks she has come up with the new idea. Roberta acts supportive and strokes Betty's huge ego. Impulsive and attention-driven, Betty begins to chat up the idea with almost everyone. Roberta watches and waits. If the idea bombs with others in the organization, Betty is blamed. If it's a good idea, Roberta will allow Betty to take some of the credit, but she'll play on the Performer's natural aversion to responsibility and assume full control of the project.

Commanders use the weaknesses of Performers. As in the example of Betty and Roberta, Commanders take advantage of the impulsiveness of Performers to float trial balloons in the organization or to try risky, unproven ideas. Performers aren't usually threatened by the control needs of the Commander as long as the person in charge exercises minimum accountability and provides opportunities for recognition.

Empathizers and Analyzers

This is another example of complementary styles that get along more by default than design. Both are introverts, content to work unnoticed in the background.

Empathizers rarely voice negative opinions and Analyzers mostly keep to themselves. However, it's not uncommon for Empathizers to team up with Analyzers to frustrate Commanders who have become dictatorial or Performers who have grown erratic and unpredictable. Empathizers and Analyzers both require an orderly, predictable work environment. They are experts at working behind the scenes to build alliances and manage the flow of information (both factual and political).

Contradictory Styles Undermine Teamwork

Some styles simply don't get along. They share nothing in common and do not understand each other. People with contradictory styles are convinced the other side is intentionally frustrating them. Put these styles together and invariably you generate conflict, mistrust, and miscommunication on your team.

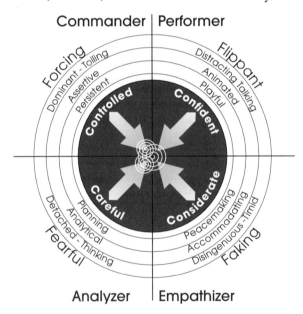

Figure 4 – Contradictory Styles

Figure 4 illustrates the contradictory behavioral styles generated by Life-Needs.

Commanders and Empathizers

What drives a wedge between Commanders and Empathizers? Commanders talk about Empathizers as "bleeding hearts." Empathizers label Commanders "cold hearted" and insensitive. Each accuses the other of having a serious character flaw.

Their Life-Needs are completely at odds with each other. The Commander is an extroverted, task-oriented individual. Commanders seldom care about the personal feelings of others. They are bottom-line decision-makers. Empathizers are introverted and people-oriented. They want people to be comfortable with them. Empathizers are not competitive, like Commanders, but value cooperation and teamwork. Commanders and Empathizers are complete opposites. They don't communicate, and tend to mistrust each other.

Performers and Analyzers

Performers and Analyzers don't work well together. The more out-of-balance the Attention and Approval Life-Needs of the individuals on this team, the more they frustrate each other. Performers are extroverted and playful while Analyzers tend to be introverted and serious. Performers ridicule Analyzers by calling them "anal-retentive" (the term has great shock value). Analyzers are convinced Performers are shallow and phony. Their styles clash because each needs exactly the Life-Need in which the other is most deficient.

Identical Extroverted Styles

Commanders don't do well with other strong Commanders. Their strong competitive nature and territorialism make the possibilities for teamwork similar to that of two male lions within close proximity of each other. They instinctively become combative. There can usually be only one true Commander on any team. If there are two, they frequently resort to Machiavellian power plays until one is forced to retreat.

The other extroverted style is the Performer. Picture two actors hamming it up on the stage, each trying to upstage the other. Put two Performers too close together and you have chaos as each tries to outdo the other and distracts anyone else within earshot.

Double Trouble

Human behavior is very complex. I developed the Five Need Theory from real-time sales research to help managers explain human behavior and teamwork variables. So far in this book, I've talked about Commanders and Empathizers and Analyzers and Performers, but people are seldom, if ever, one pure style. Since everybody possesses all Life-Needs in some mixture, most people are combinations of styles. In fact, salespeople can be comfortable in one style of behavior on the job and behave in a completely different way at home.

In this chapter, you've learned that individual styles contradict or complement each other on a team. The assumption has been that styles were embodied in different individuals. But *some people carry around conflicting styles within themselves*. They are a walking contradiction of Life-Needs. They want control and approval, attention and information. People possessed by contradictory out of balance Life-Needs are the most difficult to manage because they find it so difficult to manage themselves.

Unbalanced contradictory styles existing within the individual create two conditions, both of which have severe repercussions for personal productivity and effective teamwork. These are:

1. The Conflicted Rep; and,

2. The Double Whammy.

These conditions are admittedly difficult to spot with the naked eye. They are much more easily observed using my SalesMAP™ profile, designed specifically to detect and measure the relative strength of Life-Needs. But these double troubles are powerful influencers of sales productivity and need to be documented.

The Conflicted Rep

Each style has its opposite (see Figure 4 above). Conflicted Reps are driven by strong needs in two incompatible Life-Needs. Conflicted Reps can be either Controller-Empathizers or Performer-Analyzers.

The Team Innovator

The more common pattern is the Performer-Analyzer. The conflict arises from the extroverted, impulsive style of the Performer at odds with the introverted, detail-oriented Analyzer pattern. Performer-Analyzer salespeople often perform the role of being team innovators. They are intuitive enough to think outside the box and at the same time possess analytical skills necessary to organize their plan and market their ideas to others. Teams benefit from Team Innovators. However, when Life-Needs get too unbalanced, the innovative salesperson undermines productivity with excessive experimentation.

Ted is always thinking up new approaches to customers. He continually experiments with fresh sales openings to see which work most effectively. Finding one,

Ted uses it for a while and then abandons it as soon as he thinks of some small way to refine his presentation. Ted's manager wonders why Ted won't use the company's standard presentation materials. But Ted would rather spend hours designing new computer slide shows with animation and built-in programming than actually use the presentation to make sales. If Ted's manager ignores Ted's ideas, Ted becomes resentful and threatens to quit work for someone who appreciates his talent. What Ted actually does is to start designing still another new system.

Ted is an Innovator. He uses his analytical skills to drive his attention needs. Innovators on sales teams are difficult to manage because selling is based on repetition, doing the same things repeatedly with new prospects. Repetition is extremely difficult for Performer-Analyzers who would rather develop sales presentations than give them.

The Team Politico

The other type of Conflicted Rep is the Empathizer-Commander. This is the rarer style, showing up in less than 5% of salespeople. The Empathizer-Commander is the Team Politico. An exaggerated control need collides with the need to be universally loved and appreciated to create a behavioral style that uses people skills to amass and maintain control.

Carlos can't walk into a meeting without becoming instantly aware of the social dynamics at work in the room. He has a knack for knowing what people are thinking and feeling just by watching them. He has learned to use this sixth sense to his advantage. Carlos gets what he wants by playing people off against each other. He manipulates. One of his close friends on the sales team jokingly refers to him as Machiavelli – the 15th century author of "The Prince," a how-to book for control freaks. Carlos is never belligerent or forceful. He's a smooth operator. He makes things happen by subtle manipulation and convincing everyone that he is only looking out for their best interest. He is scheduled for a private, confidential meeting next week with the Regional VP to discuss some concerns Carlos has with his current District Manager.

Think of politicians – people who are comfortable with power, but do not threaten others with their ambition. This is the signature behavior of the Empathizer-Commander. Politicos hardly ever show up on the radar as problem producers. They are experts at staying out of trouble, working the system to their advantage. The first time many managers even notice a problem is when they discover the Team Politico has created a mutiny among the field force and manipulated the naive manager into a career-ending corner.

The agenda of the Politicos is to take over the team. Their ambition is to become the manager. Once they reach manager, they set their sites on positions higher in the organization. They are productive only as long as their output serves to move them along the chain of command. But selling is clearly secondary to managerial ambition. They excel at building strong sales teams. They are seldom impulsive and are highly self-controlled, competitive, goal-driven, and able to build rapport and loyalty with their reps.

The Double Whammy
If someone absorbs one Life-Need (that is, is unbalanced on the high end) and at the same time avoids its opposite (is unbalanced on the low end), the effect is to double the negative impact of that Life-Need. That's the "Double Whammy." Let me explain.

Lee's SalesMAP™ profile shows an extremely high Attention Need score. He also has a very, very low Information Life-Need. Both Life-Needs are unbalanced, one high and one low. In Lee's case, the conflicts inherent in these contradictory styles synergize. We know that Performers like Lee are impulsive and tend to rely more on intuition than facts for decision-making. His low Analyzer score doubles the impact of this behavior. The low Analyzer style means Lee not only craves attention, but he avoids analysis. In most people, a strong Life-Need is offset by a more balanced state in its opposite. But Lee is a Double Whammy. The contradictory Life-Needs are reinforcing the negatives of each.

Sandra's Double Whammy also involves unbalanced Attention and Information Life-Needs. In her case, however, the Analyzer is too strong and the Performer is too weak. The effect is to double the Analyzer tendency. Sandra is more comfortable with computers than people. Her strong Information need is reinforced by a strong Attention-avoidant style that makes her excessively task-oriented.

Let's move to the Empathizer-Commander pole. Bill is both a strong Empathizer and at the same time Control-avoidant. This doubles the potency of his Empathizer style. Most salespeople have a control need strong enough to tell them when it's time to stop visiting and start closing the sale. Not Bill. His productivity suffers from a terribly costly Double Whammy.

The Oppositional
Jack's Double Whammy is the most destructive of all styles, however. A strong Control need co-existing with Approval-avoidance creates the Oppositional pattern.

Oppositionals don't allow anyone to tell them what to do and they don't much care what others on the team think about them. In fact, they are likely to do the exact opposite of what they are told.

Jack arrives late and leaves early from most meetings he attends. If the expectation is to be on time and participatory, Jack does the opposite. He dresses up on casual day and wears khakis when everyone else is in a suit. Jack loves to say no. Although very effective with clients, he drives his manager crazy. Jack is openly critical, often hostile, and refuses to be coached, advised, or managed.

The conflicted needs of control and acceptance make Oppositionals somewhat more likely to abuse drugs or alcohol.

The Oppositional is not a team player. Most Commanders have a strong enough Approval need to value teamwork. A balanced approval Life-Need offsets Oppositional tendencies. But Oppositionals not only do not need the approval of others, they behave in ways that repel it. As such, they undermine teamwork in favor of a lone ranger approach.

Double Whammy patterns are the most destructive of sales productivity, especially The Oppositional. They are difficult if not impossible to manage and undermine teamwork.

Hire Performance requires keeping Double Whammies off your sales team.

Conclusion
Hire Performance demands an understanding of teamwork. Sales organizations, like individuals, are more productive when they are made up of a balance of behavioral styles. Productivity is enhanced when compatible styles synergize and reps with conflicting styles are weeded out.

Chapter 7

Designing Your Compensation Plan

You've thought through a strategic planning process necessary for Hire Performance. You've looked at your hiring philosophy and may have begun to confront your own recruitment reluctance. You know the key objective criteria for sales success, and you've been introduced to a theory for understanding both individual and team productivity.

But there's still one more topic you must address before you're ready to advertise for candidates. How will you pay your salespeople?

Your compensation package telegraphs two strategic pieces of information about you and your business to prospective candidates:

1. How important you consider the position to be in your company.

2. How much turnover you're willing to accept.

Generally speaking, "commission-only" jobs are perceived to be more expendable and therefore less attractive to the most experienced candidates. Many sales veterans prefer the unlimited income opportunity of the commission-only package, but they are a vanishing breed. If you expect reps to underwrite their own start-up costs, you limit your pool of qualified, available candidates significantly. Commission-only pay plans may lower the company's financial risk, but they guarantee higher turnover rates, particularly if you are recruiting candidates for an entry-level position.

In Europe and Australia, salaried sales positions are the norm. In the last decade, many sales organizations in the U.S. have also frowned on commission-only selling. With the advent of "customer-oriented" sales techniques, sales gurus and trainers have convinced many that commission-only selling is a conflict of interest. They contend a rep working on commission will prefer to sell what is good for the salesperson and not necessarily what is good for the customer. These assumptions are rooted in negative experiences with unethical salespeople that generate a negative attitude toward selling in general. Eliminating commission-based selling has lowered turnover in some organizations, but it has come at the price of productivity. Salaried sales jobs tend to attract less motivated, more risk-avoidant people. Building a business requires a spirit of entrepreneurship that is born in passion and nurtured by risk.

The most common sales compensation program found today in the U.S. is a combination of salary (called a "base") and commission. This pay plan gives the starting rep the security of some income while not putting a cap on his or her income potential.

Commission vs. Base Pay

So, how do you structure the plan? How much base pay? How much commission? Here are some helpful guidelines for putting together a winning pay plan for your sales team.

1. **Is the sales cycle long or short?**
   The sales cycle is the amount of time it takes a rep to move from prospecting to closing a sale. If you sell a big-ticket item, the sales cycle may last months or even a year or more. The longer it takes to go through all the steps necessary to clinch the deal the less you can rely on a commission-only pay plan. Not many salespeople can or will wait months between paychecks. Selling that takes months for "inside champions" to move the sale through many decision-making levels (called "strategic sales") require pay plans that maximize the base pay and reward outstanding production with bonuses or incentives. Commission sales work best with relatively low-dollar sales that can be made quickly and regularly.

2. **How difficult will it be to find a candidate with the necessary skills, education, or experience to do the job?**
   The more difficult the position is to fill, the less you should rely on commission. Qualifications translate into guaranteed income for salespeople.

High commissions work best for entry level, unskilled sales positions. This compensation strategy, however, almost guarantees excessive turnover. While some personalities may be inspired by the opportunity of "unlimited income," money is not the strongest motivator for mature, long-term business relationships.

3. **How long does it take the candidate to finish training and build a customer base?**
Sales organizations today spend more than three times as much on training than they did at the end of the 20th century. Extensive product lines require additional instruction. More and more 21st century jobs depend on complex technology. It is not unusual for reps to need training in computer-based reporting and relationship management programs, Internet or intranet systems, sophisticated telecommunications options, and more. It is unreasonable to expect the salesperson to shoulder the financial responsibility of learning the ropes. Long ramp-up time means you'll probably need to invest more in base pay at start-up and then gradually shift to commissions as the candidate gains skills and becomes more self-sustaining.

4. **What's the going rate? What is the most common pay plan for the position in your industry?**
You don't have to phone your competitor to discover how they pay their reps. You can get a clear picture relatively quickly by looking at job placement ads, checking out the salary requirements on resumes, and discussing the candidate's previous compensation packages.

Other resources for determining pay plans include your local Chamber of Commerce, trade publications surveys, government agencies (such as the U.S. Bureau of Labor Statistics), and job-related internet sites, many of which feature salary range finders. Salary.com tells you exactly what high, average, and low paying positions pay for a whole range of occupations in your city.

Three Commission Options
Here are three of the most popular ways salespeople are paid.

1. **Advance against commission**
   This plan pre-pays commissions to the salesperson when a sale is made. Advance plans are popular in industries where customers sign long-term payment contracts, such as insurance or security alarm sales. Although the

company may not receive full payment of the contract in advance, the company advances all or part of the commission in exchange for the salesperson's agreement to pay back the advance as the contract is fulfilled month by month. In effect, the company creates a credit arrangement with its sales force. This plan requires legal contracts that set limits on the time or the amount of advance a salesperson receives as well as specifying what happens if the salesperson leaves the company or the customer cancels payment on the contract. Advance plans require sophisticated accounting and tracking resources for sales management.

> **Benefit:** Allows salespeople to be paid during start-up.
>
> **Liability:** Company loses if sales don't match commissions.

2. Guaranteed Draw Against Commission

A "draw" pays a salary for a specified time period whether the salesperson makes any sales or not. Commissions are only paid after sales surpass a level determined by the company sufficient to pay back the company for the guaranteed base. The base pay option may continue or be discontinued. The larger the base pay, the lower the commission percentage.

> **Benefit:** Allows company to budget sales costs more effectively.
>
> **Liability:** Usually involves some salary cap that can de-motivate some salespeople.

3. Commission only

This structure usually pays a higher commission rate due to the extra risk absorbed by the salesperson. Without generating sales, the salesperson doesn't get paid. In order for this system to work, your product or service must be able to be sold quickly and frequently to a large client base.

> **Benefit:** Unlimited income potential for the motivated sales pro.
>
> **Liability:** Little company loyalty among salespeople; higher turnover.

Incentives

Incentives are an important ingredient in your overall sales compensation package. Incentives are the special bonuses and prizes awarded for exceeding expectations and quotas.

Incentives help offset any disadvantages of a pay plan. For example, to minimize turnover in a commission-only pay plan, you could structure a longevity incentive by linking commission rates to tenure. The longer a salesperson stays with the job the higher the commission rate earned.

Don't confuse bonuses and incentives. Incentives have value that exceeds their cost. Giving cash is a bonus. The value of cash equals its cost. Incentives, on the other hand, are worth more than they usually cost. Allowing the "employee of the month" to park in a favored parking space costs the company nothing, but may be quite valuable if convenient parking is at a premium.

Life-Needs give managers an easy and uncannily accurate framework for structuring incentives. If you know what motivates an individual's behavior, you can devise incentives that satisfy those basic Life-Needs. Incentives become part of the training and development program. They help salespeople get unbalanced Life-Needs back into equilibrium.

Each selling style is motivated by different incentives. For example, Empathizers with a high need for Approval value time off or social gatherings for coworkers. Performers (high need for Attention) jump through hoops for anything they can display prominently in their office (trophies, plaques) or on their person (luxury pens, jewelry). A notebook computer might thrill the excessively Analytical but mean nothing to a Commander (high need for Control). Commanders are notoriously anti-technology. Examples of powerful incentives for Commanders might be a power lunch with the company president or the chance to be on an advisory or policy board.

Incentives can include obvious employee benefits such as health insurance, credit union, or childcare. But don't overlook benefits which may not be quite so obvious, such as proximity of work to where the salesperson lives (less time in traffic), control over one's own time (more freedom), casual dress code (more relaxed atmosphere), or that you provide an office and/or secretarial help (less time spent on administration).

Think about incentives. Talk them up in your interview. They are a major selling point as you attempt to recruit top salespeople to your organization and away from your competition.

Conclusion

Most sales organizations use some kind of commission structure to pay salespeople. Higher guarantees or a generous base salary usually mean lower commission rates. On the other hand, higher commissions mean lower draws or lower base pay. Incentives should be carefully matched to the needs of candidates, as they should be an important part of your compensation package.

Chapter 8

Where to Look for Qualified Candidates

Hopefully by now you know what makes for successful salespeople and have thought through your compensation package. Now you're ready to start your search for your next top producer. But where will you look for qualified candidates for your sales position?

At this point in your recruiting, you're just like the salesperson that has completed product training and is ready to go prospecting. Hire Performance is often won or lost at this strategic point. You've analyzed and prepared. Now it's time to meet and greet. And that's prospecting!

If you are weak at trolling for talent, you will recruit salespeople who don't like to prospect either. Your recruitment reluctance will be reflected in their sales reluctance. An old proverb says, "The stream never rises higher than its source." You can't expect to build a winning sales team of contact-initiating salespeople if you yourself can't, won't, or don't beat the bushes a little. Think of this stage as earning your right to manage a winning sales team.

Managers may say it's becoming harder and harder to find great sales talent, but they're wrong. There are lots of places you can discover talented salespeople looking for a new opportunity. Certainly not all recruitment resources will be equally valuable. As they say in Texas, you'll drill some dry holes once in a while, but you'll never strike oil if you don't start drilling somewhere.

Where you decide to look for sales talent will decide two key ingredients of Hire Performance:

1. The quality and quantity of candidates who respond to your offer, and

2. The kinds of incentives you will need to offer.

For example, if you advertise in out-of-town papers or national magazines, you'll likely need to offer relocation expenses as part of your compensation package. On the other extreme, putting a "help wanted" sign in the front window of the local barber shop is not likely to produce a lot of skilled, experienced applicants.

Three rules for publicizing your position

1. Keep it simple.
Use direct, uncomplicated words to publicize your opportunity. Don't use 100 words if 50 will do. Make it easy for the recruit to contact you. Your job ad should state simply and concisely who you are, what you're looking for, and the opportunity. Spell out a clear action step for qualified candidates who want to respond to your ad. Phone. Fax. Visit. Email.

2. Keep it local.
The closer you stay to your home base, the more you'll keep advertising costs down and greatly increase your chances of finding someone who will stick with you. While Internet ads may seem really sexy and generate a lot of resumes, don't overlook low-tech options. Distribute fliers in your building or neighborhood. Try an ad in the local paper read by most people in your target market. If you can, run your ad in multiple papers. Extend your visibility by purchasing local radio and billboard ads. Only move up to regional or national sources when you've exhausted your local recruiting supply. The further from home you go, the more it will cost.

3. Target the appeal.
Dragnets are OK for cops and robbers, but not for managers trying to recruit a winning sales team. If you make your job ad too broad, you'll waste precious interviewing time weeding out unqualified applicants. Publicize your offer in terms that reflect exactly how you like to work and what you expect in candidates. Learn to talk the language of the person you want to attract. There are more details on exactly how to do this in the next chapter. But for now, let's review some recruitment sources and evaluate a few strengths and weaknesses of each.

Free Recruitment Sources

Don't overlook virtually cost-free options you have right under your nose for publicizing your position. Here are just a few:

1. **Personal and Professional Referrals**

   Preparing to write this chapter, I surveyed a number of top-money professional recruiters with the question "What's the best source of leads for recruiting great salespeople?"

   Their answer was unanimous: your own network of contacts. Why? Because it meets the three rules for publicizing your position – it's simple, it's local, and targets the appeal.

   Ask your friends for the names of sharp people they know. It doesn't matter if the people they recommend are looking to make a change or not. Build a list of talented people from colleagues and friends you know and respect.

   Friends aren't the only people in your sphere of influence. Our lives are populated with many outstanding people in their fields, all of whom are a storehouse of potential leads. Talk to your banker, your insurance agent, or your accountant, professionals you know and trust. Describe what you're looking for in a phone call, email or personal note to them. Attach a copy of your sizzling recruitment ad. If they give you a referral, ask permission to use their names. You intensify your recruiting appeal considerably if you can introduce yourself to a prospect by saying, "I was talking to John Smith at the bank the other day and he tells me you're really a go-getter. I'd like to talk to you about an opportunity."

   Never forget, "The best jobs aren't in the paper." It's true. The pros will tell you. Regardless of what kind of selling or recruiting you do, there's absolutely no substitute for personal and professional networking.

2. **Local professional organizations.**

   Other often-overlooked sources of free contacts are professional and service organizations in your community. Civic clubs and social groups offer space on bulletin boards and in their newsletters. Don't overlook women's professional groups as well as the traditional service organizations in your community.

Religious groups (churches, synagogues, fraternal organizations, etc.) are another fertile field for leads. Pastors, priests, and rabbis know good people in their congregations who may be looking for exactly the opportunity you could be offering.

3. **Local schools and institutions of higher learning.**
High schools, colleges, universities, and technical schools offer career counseling and job placement services to their graduates. Visit local campuses. Get to know the people in charge of job placement. Ask about job fairs and other appropriate ways you can work with these campuses to publicize your opportunity. At the very least, ask to post your recruitment ad on a bulletin board.

4. **Public employment bureaus.**
Visit the folks at your local or state employment service. Many of these offices are connected to the U.S. Employment Service that provides hiring resources to businesses like yours. Your only outlay to tap into this vast network is a little time and effort.

5. **Major employers in your community laying off workers.**
Merger mania, downsizing and reorganization create corporate instability in the marketplace. Companies forced to retrench lay-off quality employees. Frequently, these firms hire outplacement specialists who look for community partners to help employees find new work. Identify yourself to these professionals and be sure to include them in your recruitment network.

6. **What about recruiting your competitor's reps?**
This question always comes up in our Hire Performance seminars and invariably prompts a great deal of discussion. There is no simple answer. My personal opinion is that your best strategy about recruiting competitor's reps will depend on your industry and your management style. Highly specialized positions requiring experienced candidates virtually guarantee some employee raiding.

One manager in the credit card services industry tells about an interesting tactic. He answers the newspaper ads of his competitors, pretending to be looking for a job. He says it gets him in front of experienced people (yes, the people interviewing him for the job) who are often surprisingly eager to learn of a better opportunity when they discover the true purpose for his appointment. Not everyone could carry off this bit of chutzpah, but it works for him.

You probably won't be surprised to know that his management style is that of the Commander-Performer. Recruiters with high control needs find guerilla techniques like this immensely satisfying.

Going behind enemy lines has pluses and minuses. On the plus side, you not only find experienced salespeople with contacts, you temporarily deal your rival a severe setback by stealing a productive player off the opposing team. On the negative side, you create legal tangles for yourself if the salesperson is encumbered by a non-compete clause in the previous employer's contract. And something else to think about: there's no guarantee that a top salesperson in one organization will automatically repeat his or her success in your company. Successful selling involves more than just the selling style of the rep. The previous environment may have supplied a more compatible management style, corporate culture, business climate, etc.

Raiding the competition's talent is done every day. But remember – what goes round comes round.

For-Hire Recruitment Sources

For-hire recruitment sources usually will generate more leads more quickly than word-of-mouth networking, but very often they aren't worth what you have to pay. In your quest to find qualified candidates, you can spend considerable time and money collecting a pile of resumes. While gratified that you're getting a lot of bang for your advertising buck, can you afford to spend hours sorting through worthless resumes?

Here are three for-hire sources listed in order of their productivity.

1. Newspaper ads

Most managers routinely use print advertising sources to recruit salespeople. Help wanted ads in local or regional newspapers usually attract a large number of applicants. One sales manager received over 750 resumes in response to his weekend ad run in a large metropolitan paper. But of all those responses, less than five matched his profile, and of those five not one made it past an initial interview.

Newspaper ads will get noticed, especially in the Sunday papers. But this shotgun approach can waste a lot of time for recruiters. If you use newspaper classifieds, run ads only in local newspapers. Anyone who has to commute more than 45 minutes a day is very likely to quit for a job closer to home. Your ad copy must be sizzling and succinct. You must be willing to pay the price for an effective ad campaign. If you can't afford to run an ad of at least two column inches for two or three weeks, you're probably wasting your money.

Resist the temptation to publish a fax number and request resumes in your newspaper ad. Underline and highlight that statement. When recruiting a winning sales team, you're looking for people with the drive and determination to initiate contact. We know from years of research that contact initiation is the only proven predictor of success in sales. So, make the action line of your ad something that requires the candidate taking initiative to contact you.

Bring your resume in person to ....

Call today for an appointment ....

Anybody who won't call and leave a message or show up in person for an interview isn't likely to take initiative with your customers either.

If using the phone is important to the sales position you're advertising, require candidates to leave a detailed phone message telling about themselves and why they are interested in your opportunity. Listen for enthusiasm and energy in their voices. Can they put together an intelligent sentence? Can they "sell" you on an interview? What's their phone "presence"?

If canvassing or cold calling is important to success in your business, your ad should have a call to action to show up for an in-person interview. Use the employment process itself to screen out applicants who are weak in the one key competency you know spells success in sales – making contacts.

2. Trade Publications

In addition to local newspapers, you can also advertise in industry trade publications. This strategy will be more appropriate for business-to-business sales situations than consumer-oriented selling. Depending on the industry and type of journal, ads in trade publications may cost more than ads in local papers and will broaden your dragnet beyond the local scene. "Trades" are most appropriate when you require an on-going supply of highly skilled applicants.

One negative about advertising in trade magazines is the long lead time it may take to get your ad placed. Trades may be published only once a quarter. If you have a long lead time to fill a senior-level position, these publications may be very helpful.

3. **Headhunters**
   Other for-hire recruitment sources include professional headhunters and employment sites on the Internet.

   These resources work best for far-flung sales operations spread over many locations that are continuously recruiting. Large organizations may find professional recruitment services cost-effective. Medium-sized and small businesses seldom have the benefit of such economies of scale.

   Recruiters who work on a commission-only basis are called "contingency recruiters," as opposed to fee-based recruiters. You pay the recruiter's fee if you hire the individual referred to you by the headhunter. In reality, most headhunters are little more than resume collectors. The advantage for you is that you only have to deal with one other individual in the early stages of the selection process instead of many job candidates. But you must ultimately do the interviewing and make the final call. A huge negative associated with using hired guns is that you cede control of the selection process to someone who has little if any stake in your long-term business success.

   As a general rule, I suggest starting your recruitment with the free, local sources and only resort to for-hire recruitment sources if your own serious efforts at networking fail to produce a pool of qualified candidates.

Conclusion
Your best bet for finding qualified candidates is through your own networking efforts. If you must use for-hire recruitment services, be sure to keep it simple, keep it local, and target the appeal.

Chapter 9

How to Write a Sizzling Recruitment Ad

The best way to learn about writing a good recruitment ad is to spend some time reading and analyzing recruitment ads. Find last Sunday's classifieds. Turn to the "Sales" section. As you browse, pay special attention to the ads that immediately catch your eye. Why are these more attractive than other ads? Why do you read some and skip over others? Do some ads seem to have more credibility than others? If so, why?

Size Matters

Before candidates read one word of your ad, they've already formed an opinion of your company from the appearance and size of your ad. In recruitment ads, the media is the message.

Ancient artists were required to paint kings larger than life. To modern eyes, the perspective seems all wrong. But those primitive monarchs knew bigger was better, or at least more important. People instinctively look first at what is largest on the page. It's the way our brains work. It's also the way classified ads work. In most newspapers, larger job notices get placed first. So, when both size and position work for you, your ad screams, "I'm important. Pay attention to me."

Along with size, the appearance of your ad either invites or repels readers. Our brains intuitively dislike complexity and confusion. So, people will be more attracted to your ad if you don't cram too much information into your ad. Empty space is more attractive to the brain than clutter. Notice the use of "white space" in the employment ads that caught your eye. If you must include a lot of fine print in your ad, be sure your headline and your main recruiting points stand out by surrounding them with white space.

The Art of Advertising

Big ads attract attention, particularly if they contain artwork or photos. The human eye is conditioned to look at faces first. Until you can afford some of those big name celebrity endorsements, you may not have famous faces to draw attention to your ads. That's OK. Any photo of smiling, attractive people will be more likely to get noticed than ads without pictures of people.

One company tripled the response rate to its recruitment ad by adding its corporate logo. The logo wasn't particularly noteworthy. As with faces, the brain is instinctively attracted to symbols. By adding images, white space draws the eye to the logo as an easy focal point. The brain is always looking for clues to simplifying the chaos coming at it from the environment. The brain directs attention first of all to large symbols before trying to interpret small ones (such as words).

Match Values to Needs

So far I haven't said anything about the content of your recruitment ad. The omission is intentional. Usually it's the case that the words you use are secondary to the size, placement and attractive design of the ad. If prospects don't notice the ad and gain a positive impression of what you have to offer, the chances of their reading the ad are small. If the design doesn't match the copy, your credibility suffers and the response rate plummets. Once you've got the reader's attention, your ad's got to sizzle if you're going to "sell" the reader.

Let's revisit what we've learned about why people buy things. Sales happen when you fill a need with something the customer is convinced has value. That means before a sale takes place, three things have to happen:

1. You have to be in front of a customer;

2. You have to know what the customer needs; and,

3. You have to persuade the customer of the value of your product or service to satisfy that need.

Let's apply these same three principles to writing a recruitment ad. First, you've got to decide where and how your ad will get in front of prospective salespeople. You have to target your market. Once you know whom you're trying to reach, you'll have a much better idea about how you can reach them. Determining the medium, size, placement, and scheduling of your ad campaign flows from knowing your audience. If you live in a metropolitan area, you may need to target your ad to the readership of one paper more than another.

Second, your ad must create a need or bring an unconscious need above the threshold of awareness.

And third, your ad must persuade readers that what you have to offer will satisfy those needs. The deeper and more personal the need you can address and satisfy, the more likely you are to generate a response.

By now, you should be getting a clearer idea of what you value as well as some of the basic needs of salespeople you need to address. You can once again use the Life-Needs model to demystify the process of matching values to needs. If your ad can subliminally addresses Life-Needs, candidates will find your ad more enticing and they will be more motivated to talk with you about your opportunity. And that's the number one function of an ad.

Life-Needs create your selling style. What do you need – Attention, Control, Approval, Information, Stability, or are you one of those rare people who are a balanced combination of all five? Most people are not dominated by one Life-Need but are influenced by a combination. For example, you might be a Perfectionist Commander (high Information needs compensated for by strong, but balanced Control need) or an Intuitive Empathizer (low Information need, but high Approval need). Whatever the Life-Needs that dominate, if you can broadly identify your selling style, you'll also know the core values you bring to recruiting a winning sales team.

If your selling style is that of an Analyzer, you not only thrive on information, you also value organization and efficiency. Empathizers need approval, and they value teamwork and openness. If you're a Performer, you like people to pay attention to you. Performers also value spontaneity and an ability to think on one's feet. Commanders need control and value loyalty and decisiveness. Whatever your style, it should shape the ad campaign you run because it reflects your basic business values.

Tailoring the ad to reflect your style is more important if you are also going to manage the salesperson than if you do not interact on a daily basis with the person you recruit. Professional recruiters will want to pay attention to how their Life-Needs can skew their perception and overly influence the objectivity of the interview process. But the sales manager who recruits his or her team should be careful and intentional about building any recruitment ad around his personal management and/or selling style.

Your selling style and its associated values will also help you attract some types of candidates to your job while putting off other types. If you're trying to build a winning team, you don't want everyone responding to your ad. If a baseball team desperately needs pitchers, scouts shouldn't be wasting time interviewing shortstops or outfielders. In the same way, you want the right people responding to your recruitment invitation. And the right people are those who share your values and match not only the skill needs of the position, but also match the management style of their front-line coach. Remember, some styles work well together. Other styles make sparks fly.

Writing a sizzling recruitment ad requires paying careful attention to the values you communicate and the styles you're most likely to attract. You want to attract people with styles that are compatible to your own and discourage candidates who bring incompatible styles to your team.

How Recruitment Ads Communicate Values

OK, so what's all this got to do with writing a sizzling, succinct recruitment ad? Everything!

If you're aware of your style, you know the kind of people with whom you are likely work best and those who will frustrate you. Design words and pictures which appeal to deep pre-conscious needs of those you want and need to attract. You want to attract candidates with a style compatible to your own or to others on your team.

If you have a strong Commander style, your recruitment ad should NOT emphasize concepts like teamwork and cooperation. These values will mostly attract Empathizers.

My Commander style makes it very hard for me to work well with Empathizers. When I'm looking for someone to hire, I intentionally speak in short, stabbing phrases. I don't use a lot of inflection in my voice. This style tends to keep Empathizers away.

Your recruitment ads begin to match values and needs as they appeal to the individual's basic Life-Needs with words and pictures. Remember – you don't want to hire individuals with out-of-control Life-Needs. Even salespeople with a balanced selling style will have a slight preference for one or two styles. Here are some examples that show how words and images can attract and appeal to specific styles.

If you need a salesperson to impress others and tell your story, attract Performers with appeals to recognition, prestige and glamour. Picture young, energetic, well-dressed, laughing people in your ad. Always start the ad with the word "YOU" in large, bold letters. Appeal to the Performer's sense of fun. Position your opportunity as prestigious with lots of opportunity for recognition. Performers are drawn to money because it represents the enjoyment of life.

> *Example: You can have a blast marketing our world-renowned product to high-end homeowners. If you're an energetic, dynamic free thinker, we want to see you.*

If you need a self-starting salesperson who doesn't require a lot of oversight, attract Commanders with appeals to control, promotion, and privilege. Here's one interesting discovery I've made about Commanders. They seem to be instinctively attracted to negative advertising. You'll get their attention best by starting your ads with negative words such as "Don't," "You can't," and "Never." Appeal to their sense of duty and suspiciousness. Position your opportunity as demanding with the opportunity for advancement.

> *Example: Don't read this ad unless you're one tough-minded closer who can handle responsibility that would destroy most salespeople.*

One note of caution: Be ready for the kind of people who will answer an ad like this.

If you need a salesperson who is careful and conscientious, attract Analyzers with ads that ask questions rather than make statements. Include lots of facts and figures, graphs and charts, maps and details. Small print acts like an aphrodisiac for Analyzers. Position your opportunity as a problem to be solved. Be sure to mention benefits and company stability.

> *Example: Are you looking for salary plus bonus plus benefits? We're a solid, stable company looking for an expert to solve our customer's problems.*

If you need a salesperson to build relationships and service existing accounts, appeal to Empathizers by emphasizing teamwork and personal caring in your ads. Use words like "us" and "our." Soften the hard edges. Use pictures of people working together and smiling.

> *Example: Our close-knit team needs a sensitive individual to service existing accounts and invite new clients to partner with our company.*

The more you know about your selling style and the kind of relational skills necessary to sell your product or service, the better, more effective ad you'll write. By targeting needs you will communicate at a subliminal level that will single out and strengthen the appeal to your ideal candidate.

EEOC Guidelines

Be careful to avoid mentioning anything in your ad about race, religion, color, gender, age, physical abilities, or other factors which may be considered discriminatory. Not only are such biases illegal in today's workplace, they are also bad for business. Be sure any and all requirements outlined in your recruitment ad are clearly job-related. Keep the focus on what people DO, not what they ARE. If you satisfy these requirements you qualify to end your ad with the phrase, "Equal Opportunity Employer."

Ads Communicate Your Uniqueness

If repetition is the key to learning, read this next sentence at least three times. **Target your recruitment ad to the values and needs of your prime candidates.**

Additionally, your ad should tell candidates one or two unique facts about you, your company or product, or work environment. Tell them what differentiates you from your competition. Hammer these distinctive factors home every chance you get. You're further ahead stating one unique benefit about your work (flexible hours, casual dress code, location of your company) than you are publicizing a laundry list of trumped-up hyperbole ("unlimited income," "chance of a lifetime," "easiest job you'll ever have").

Publish the income range of the position as well as the compensation package (commission, salary plus bonus, etc.).

"Commission only; average first year income $38-42K."

"Starting monthly draw during 3 months of training $1.2K; full commission thereafter."

Realistic income estimates will attract more genuinely qualified candidates. Overstated claims may entice some gullible folks to contact you, and you may even get some of them to sign up. But you come out ahead financially by telling the truth up-front rather than incurring the high costs of job turnover from the disillusioned and disaffected.

Remember – the purpose of the ad is to find candidates who match your needs, not generate a pile of resumes.

Action Line

Perhaps the most important part of any recruitment ad is the call to action. What is it you want prospective candidates to do? The action line needs to be spelled out clearly and precisely.

You have five basic action choices:
- Come
- Call
- Fax
- Email
- Mail

What your ad asks candidates to do predicts the kind of response you get. Your action line can work for you or against you.

If you want to get a lot of responses, publish a fax number or an e-mail address and ask for resumes. These action lines require the least initiative or commitment. Asking candidates to mail resumes ups the ante a little, as the job seeker has to invest the price of a postage stamp and a trip to the mailbox.

Don't ask candidates to call unless you have voice mail. Answering calls from an ad is a huge time and energy trap, especially if you're a small or one-person operation. You can't interview and take calls at the same time. There are other less obvious problems with this method as well. What if a good candidate reaches a busy signal while you're explaining your opportunity for the umpteenth time? It could be a very expensive missed opportunity.

Don't write off the phone entirely, though. One top recruiter in the mortgage loan business ends recruiting ads for telesales candidates with an action line to call and leave a five minute voice-mail message.

"On my message, I introduce the company, describe the position and what we're looking for, and then ask them to tell me about themselves and why we might want to interview them," he explains.

"Since the core competency of our job is using the phone, I learn a lot more from their voice mail messages than I do from a resume. Besides, the people who aren't comfortable on the phone either hang up or never even bother to call. That saves me a lot of time and wasted effort."

Here's an important principle to remember: **always relate your ad's call to action to the skills and initiative required by the job**. The more commitment your action line requires, the fewer responses you get. But the candidates who do respond will usually be of much better quality.

Asking a candidate to show up in person not only weeds out those with little initiative, it also says right up front – initiating contact is the most important skill required for success in this position.

In general, you should avoid asking for resumes. Sure, everybody wants to see a good response from an advertising investment, but a blizzard of creative writing is hardly the best measure of an ad's success. In fact, the less your job requires writing and organizational skills, the less you should rely on written resumes.

Asking sales candidates to send resumes elicits only low energy, low commitment responses. It invites many of the merely curious to distract you from finding qualified candidates with more drive and initiative. You're hiring a salesperson, not a librarian. Use the hiring process to filter out the unmotivated and non-serious candidates.

Conclusion

The well-written recruitment ad describes not only the nature of the job, but also communicates to candidates at verbal and non-verbal levels important messages about your values. Recruitment ads should be designed and written to target the needs of complementary selling styles. Honest ads minimize costly turnover. Use an action line to filter out the unmotivated by requiring a response that is critical to job performance.

Chapter 10

Getting What You Really Need from Resumes

Reading and evaluating resumes is always part of recruiting a winning sales team, but Hire Performance demands that you **do not rely heavily on the resume**. Resumes are often constructed to conceal much more than they reveal. With a little help, though, you can dig out the critical information you need. You have to learn to how to get at the truth that all too often lies buried between the lines.

First Read: The Scan Sort

Don't read all the resumes you receive. Your time is too valuable. Start by simply scanning resumes for one or two items that stand out. This is called the "scan sort" because you can eliminate many candidates with a quick inspection of the resume. You'll be able to discard many resumes with just a quick once-over. Some will be sloppy and unprofessional. Others will quickly reveal a person without enough experience or education. All the resumes that survive this initial once-over can be prioritized later according to your hiring profile. Scan sorting is a skill you develop with practice.

Get three cardboard boxes. Label or color them "green," "yellow," and "red." In the green box put all the resumes that pass your initial scan criteria. Toss your obvious rejects into the red box. The yellow box is for everyone else –"a definite maybe."

Don't bother printing e-mailed resumes. Peruse them on your monitor. Don't waste time and resources when you don't have to. Instead of boxes, create folders on your computer into which you scan sort the resumes you receive. Scan the page quickly without getting bogged down in details.

Three rhyming words guide your initial resume scan sort: neat, complete, and meet.

1. **Is it *neat*?**
   Neatness correlates highly with conscientiousness. Sloppy resumes point to someone who isn't careful or who didn't take the time to do something properly. If you sell a technically sophisticated product, a neat resume will be a vital clue to spotting quality candidates.

   Neat means clean – not covered with coffee stains or great globs of correction fluid. Neat also means correct. If your initial scan reveals obvious misspelled words and grammatical mistakes, you're looking at a candidate who is either in too big a hurry or who may require additional training.

   Neat does not necessarily mean flashy. I'm a sucker for the resumes of Performers. It's easy to get distracted by the glamour-puss pictures plastered on the front, the attention-grabbing color and expensive paper. Good resumes can also be simple and neat. Beware of the flashy look with lots of spelling errors or inconsistent formatting. It could indicate a candidate who relies on charm to cover up mistakes.

2. **Is it *complete* (and concise)?**
   Long resumes usually mean one of three things.

   1. The candidate is an exceptionally experienced individual responding to an ad that was overly general.

   2. The candidate has a tough time focusing on priorities.

   3. The candidate is likely a big-time Analyzer with out-of-balance Information needs.

   You can expect longer resumes if you're trolling for skilled, experienced candidates. If your recruitment ad asks for resumes, require that they be concise, one-page summaries. This not only saves you time but gives you a clue about the candidate's ability to focus and set priorities.

Complete also means no gaps in employment or educational history. Gaps often mean something is being covered up. The candidate doesn't want you to know about what was happening during that time period. Spotting gaps does not require a lot of time spent reading details. If your quick scan reveals obvious missing information, don't put that resume with your top candidates. Don't get bogged down in too many details, worrying if you'll miss something in a resume. If it's worthwhile, you'll catch it later when you unpack the green box and the yellow box.

3. **Do skills and background *meet* your criteria?**
Someone with experience in your industry might be a better candidate than the rookie with no background or training. However, don't assume all experienced candidates automatically match your profile. Similarly, you shouldn't be too quick to disqualify an applicant with a background that may not exactly fit the sketch of your ideal candidate. The yellow box is for those resumes that have caught your interest for some reason. It's not even important at the scan sort stage for you to know why you put a resume in the yellow box. Things can be interesting without necessarily being good or bad, right or wrong.

A quick way to determine if a resume meets your criteria is to look for the candidate's job objective. Not all resumes contain an objective, but those that do will usually put it right at the top of the page. Scan the career objective first. If it is obvious that the objective doesn't match the position you've got, dump it in the red box.

After you've completed your initial scan sort, save the resumes in the green and yellow boxes. Trash everything in the red box without a second thought.

The Closer Read

The scan sort whittles down the task of resume reading to a more manageable size. The next stage is the closer read. Begin with resumes in the green box. If you have sorted e-mailed resumes, at this point print the ones that belong in the green box. Put the yellow box aside for the time being. Your focus for the closer read is only on your best candidates.

Photocopy the resumes in your green box. You're going to make comments and notations on the resume, so keep a clean original as backup.

As you read the green box resumes from candidates who made your initial cut, circle or highlight anything that leaps off the page at you. Positive or negative, it could be an important clue to the individual's values and selling style. Make notes of your concerns and questions in the margins of the resume. Don't worry about making any final decisions at this stage.

You're now ready to gather business intelligence on your candidates. Here are clues that emerge from typical sales resumes.

Work and education history

Background and education can help you determine a couple of important facts about your candidate.

1. Does the individual's background match the requirements you need? Does this person have experience with the kind of market she/he will be selling to? What does his/her education tell you about career aspirations? If your company sells pharmaceuticals to doctors and pharmacists, a candidate with only a high school diploma may not be the best fit.

2. Work and education history can also provide a heads-up about the individual's stability. Did she finish school? How long did he stay at his last couple of jobs? Obviously, young people just beginning a career are going to show less workplace stability than someone with lots of experience. If you spot a pattern of changing addresses or jobs every six to eight months with an experienced candidate, it's a pretty safe bet this rep won't be around your company long either.

While we're on the subject, let's examine a question that many recruiters ask and upon which they disagree. How much mobility is too much? Some managers say a candidate who stays in any job for more than three or four years may not have enough initiative. This really depends on the industry and the state of the economy. In the unprecedented growth market of the 90's, good candidates moved on every six months as opportunities exploded and businesses couldn't get enough workers. In the aftermath of the dot bomb and telecommunications meltdown, jobs became scarcer. People are less likely to change jobs.

As a rule, 18 months to 3 years in a sales position is about average. If your candidate is changing jobs every six months to a year, you probably need to ask some questions about stability. Three years or more in an entry level job or 5 years in the same managerial position may indicate complacency or risk-avoidance.

When you evaluate a candidate's experience, you can also get a feel for the amount and types of training that may be required. The more you invest in training your sales team the less you can afford to hire a job jumper.

Hobbies

Hobbies listed on sales resumes generate a lot of disagreement among sales recruiters. Some see hobbies as a distraction from selling. Others believe listing hobbies offers evidence of a well-rounded individual.

Probably both are right. If the candidate has included hobbies or outside interests in a resume, there's a reason. For the inexperienced candidate, it may be to fill up space on the page. Or, it could be a talking point your candidate wishes to raise in a potential interview.

You gather two important pieces of intelligence from your candidate's list of hobbies: outside distractions and energy level.

First, shy away from candidates with hobbies requiring on-going commitments of time and energy. Coaching little league, serving on the school board, or getting active in politics are wonderful avocations, but these hobbies play havoc with a career. They take huge blocks of time and often zap the energy and focus demanded by sales. Consumer sales, such as insurance, cars, or security systems, usually demand that reps sell at night and on weekends. Be sure candidate hobbies don't conflict. If candidates are forced to choose between hobbies they've learned to enjoy and a new job, they may make some adjustments in the short run, but ultimately the hobbies will squeeze out the job.

Hobbies also indicate a person's energy level. When it comes to top producing salespeople, active hobbies like swimming, bike riding, or jogging are best. There's nothing wrong with a candidate whose resume lists Internet surfing, computer games, reading or other passive hobbies, but there's a strong correlation between active hobbies and career stamina. Circle these items and follow-up in the interview.

Track Record
Be impressed with resumes that provide real sales numbers and not just titles and duties. Put these in the green box right away. Specificity is a strong sign that your candidate knows the importance of setting goals and being accountable for production. Even so, citing sales numbers is not necessarily proof that your applicant was directly responsible for such success. Could be the individual is claiming success for a team effort. Still, a clearly spelled out track record indicates your candidate knows that sales is ultimately about the bottom line. Circle the sales numbers as a topic for follow-up.

References
Contacting previous employers is becoming increasingly problematic. Recent precedent-setting lawsuits leave employers legally vulnerable for unfavorable recommendations that may contribute to a candidate being passed over for a job. So the most you'll get from contacting previous employers is verification of the dates of employment and perhaps a job title.

References on resumes are virtually worthless. Most people only give the names of people prepared to sing their praises, but we can look at candidate references from a different angle to uncover some critical clues about potential performance. For example, is the candidate willing to provide references? If not, why? What kind of references are they? Are they personal or professional? Is there anyone from a previous place of employment on the list? If so, is it a supervisor or a friend? The absence of professional references could merely indicate a lack of experience, but it might also be a clue that the candidate did not leave on the best of terms.

Always check out a candidate's references. Here are some tips that should help you avoid trouble and get the information you really need.

1. **Identify yourself and the purpose of your call.**
   "Hello, Mr. Jones, my name is Dave Barnett with The Barnett Group. I'm calling because Joe Candidate listed you as a reference on his resume." Then shut up and gauge the immediate reaction. Does the reference want to talk about the candidate? Is she open to your call? Does she sound excited and enthusiastic, or do you sense apathy, confusion or restraint? Those first few seconds speak volumes about the quality of this reference.

One reference I called took a few seconds to respond to my inquiry.

"Sally SalesRep listed you as a reference and I'd like to talk with you. Is this a bad time?" I asked.

"No," the voice on the other end of the phone said slowly.

I confirmed that Sally had worked as a rep in the company for the past couple of years. Then he volunteered, "Sally. Hmmm. Yea, I guess you could say she did pretty well. Good salesperson. Sure."

That slight hesitation, that little phrase "I guess," told me more about the quality of the reference than anything she said. He was trying to talk himself into giving Sally a positive reference. The words were there, but not the enthusiasm.

2. **Begin by putting the reference at ease.**
"I'm merely following up on Joe's references and I wonder if you would you feel comfortable telling me a little about how well you know Joe."

Include this step if you're calling on a small business owner, frontline manager, or any non-HR professional. These business people must be a jack-of-all-trades. They have lots of good information, but they may have read an article about businesses getting in trouble for giving bad referrals. Sometimes they're just too busy to talk. In those cases, they'll usually ask you to call back. Be aware that many small businesses are wary about references because they fear getting themselves or the candidate in trouble.

If you recognize any hesitation on the reference's part to speak openly or candidly, and the reference hasn't arranged a time to call back due to busyness, politely terminate the call. That hesitation may indicate an issue between the candidate and this reference that could become a problem if pursued. It's just not worth it. In general, references will only give you positive information. Don't embarrass them or yourself by putting them in situations where they are forced to speak negatively.

3. **Ask open-ended questions.**
"I'm sure you know how important it is to follow up on references. Why do you think Joe included you on his list?"

Don't ask the reference directly for opinions about the candidate's personality, character, or personal preferences. Legally, you could be at risk if you use the reference's opinion to disqualify an individual from a job, so don't waste your time asking. You could expose the unwitting reference to similar legal issues if you were found to have induced them to give a negative reference for which they are held liable.

If a former employer hesitates to speak openly or candidly, withdraw the questions about performance and simply confirm the dates of employment and inquire about the candidate's title when employed.

4. **If the reference volunteers negative information about the candidate, affirm the absolute confidentiality of your conversation.**
Say something along these lines. *"Thank you for volunteering that information. I want to reassure you that your opinions will be held in the strictest confidence and your recommendations are only one of several sources of information we're using to select a person for the position."*

Document your reply by keeping it on file with the resume of the candidate for a year. You may wish to send it to your lawyer or legal department. Discuss the issue with competent legal counsel to be sure you handle all employment issues according to the laws of your state as well as federal regulations.

Verbs
At the risk of sounding like an English teacher, you can learn a lot about a candidate by reviewing the verbs on the resume. As you read the resume, circle all the action words. Verbs express behavior. What do they communicate? Are the verbs active (sold, managed, led, built, etc.) or passive (assisted, learned, was exposed to, etc.)? Is the applicant action-oriented or thinking-oriented? Are the words you've circled the kinds of behaviors you need for a candidate to succeed?

Prepare For Your Interview
The close read of the resumes in the green box prepares you for the next step – your employment interview. You should be prepared for at least two interviews

with every serious candidate. Three is probably better. Study the resumes in your green box closely before your first interview (if possible). If your call to action was to bring their resumes with them to an initial interview, you'll need to study it in more detail before your second get-together.

As you prepare for the in-depth interview, make notes. Write down questions you need to ask. Hopefully the insights gained from this book will make critical issues leap off the page at you.

You've gone to a lot of effort to think through your needs, plan your strategy, and set standards. Don't throw it all away at this point in the hiring process by relying on intuition.

Sales managers agonize when they must invest time and money to train salespeople to master a skill that they immediately forget in the heat of a sales call. You train your reps to follow a sales script to guide their presentation. They practice the script to perfection. But in the excitement of the actual sales call, they don't apply anything that they've learned.

That's where you are right now in your quest for Hire Performance. It's time to transfer training into practice. You've worked out a plan in previous chapters, and now you've got to stick with it. You must be selective. Even if you receive a smaller response from your ad than you hoped, you can't rush into hiring just anybody. In fact, a minimum response means you have to be more selective, more careful about those who may at first appear to be your top candidates. Better to ask the tough questions now before you invite this person on your team and put him on the payroll. Remember, every salesperson you interview puts your reputation and the future of your enterprise on the line. Compromise now and you might never discover the secret to recruiting a winning sales team.

Technicolor Resumes

OK, you're still rummaging through the green box. Read each resume in that box several times. Use color markers to prep for the interview, circling or highlighting items that you want to talk about. Be careful to avoid using colors that could telegraph too much inside information to the candidate, like red for bad or green for good. Yellow works well for items that need clarification, such as gaps in the timeline, time consuming hobbies, and questions about references. Yellow means "ask about this."

Obvious pluses in the candidate's background and/or skills can be circled in light blue highlighter. He may live close by, so circle the address. If the applicant worked in the industry for a number of years, circle it in blue. If the candidate shows good job stability, write "Stability" in the margin and circle it with blue. Perhaps you'll spot obvious elements of a selling style. Make notes using ANZ for Analyzer, PRF Performer, CMD Commander, EMP Empathizer. Scribbled in blue means that styles could be a plus; written in yellow means it could be an area of concern that needs to be verified.

Knowing your own style as a recruiter helps you understand your own biases when reading resumes. Commanders have a natural tendency to find lots of yellows and very few blues because Commanders criticize more than they compliment. If you're a Commander, discipline yourself to always make one blue mark for every yellow comment on your Technicolor resumes.

As you might imagine, Empathizing recruiters don't use yellow markers very much. They'll use up four blue markers for every yellow one because they're more comfortable giving compliments than being critical. Their need for approval generates a more accepting approach. Empathizers should develop the opposite discipline to that of the Commander – one yellow for every two blues.

Now, you Analyzers are already getting into this, devising better colors, more colors, using different symbols. Be careful that you don't spend more time analyzing than interviewing. You don't get paid to R&D the perfect the resume coloring system. Your goal is Hire Performance.

Yellow? Blue? It's all too complicated for Performers. Attention-driven people are notorious for only hearing what they want to hear. They've relied on their intuitive abilities for so long it's difficult for them to approach recruitment in any systematic way. In that case, this book might look good on the shelf next to all the rest of the unread bestsellers by celebrity gurus.

Be alert to the implications of your style as you read resumes. Be honest with yourself. Honesty is your best bet for recruiting a winning sales team.

If you follow this system for reading, prioritizing, and color coding resumes, it will be easy to know whom you should contact first. They are in the green box, and their resumes have more blue than yellow highlighting. Demote those with the fewest blue markings to the yellow box and forget about them for right now. Yellow stands for "back-ups." You are only interested in yellow box resumes after you've exhausted all those in the green box. If you do need to dip into the yellow box in the future, start again with the Technicolor resumes. They stand out because you've already determined their value to your sales efforts. Unmarked resumes in the yellow box were your lower priorities from the initial scan sort. Don't forget you may have more yellow box resumes on your computer that you'll need to print.

The more resumes you receive, the more critical it will be to implement a systematic way of dealing with all that paper. Even if you're a small start-up operation and you receive only a few resumes, it's never too soon to start building the disciplines, habits, and skills that contribute to Hire Performance.

Conclusion

Resumes can conceal as much they reveal. This chapter details a two-step process for getting at the information you need from candidate resumes. Step one – prioritize candidates by a brief scan-sort technique. Step two – check references appropriately. Step three – read closely top priority resumes, using a color marker system for identifying concerns and complements you might use in an interview.

Chapter 11

The First Interview

A recent survey of recruiters found that preparing for the first face-to-face meeting was the most difficult part of the job. Analyzers and Empathizers probably feel the most anxiety and apprehension: Analyzers, because they never feel they have enough information to carry off a good interview; and Empathizers, because they need to be liked so much they dread evaluating people and rejecting any candidate.

Does interviewing intimidate you? It shouldn't.

How Effective Are Interviews Really?

Recruiters tense up at the interview stage because they convince themselves the interview is *the critical point* in the selection process. Some recruiters should feel nervous because they haven't planned what they're going to say or do in the first interview. They leave everything to chance and gut-feel.

Candidates who are well coached in interview skills also erode the value of interviews. Job seekers may have more experience interviewing than the recruiter, especially if the manager is new at the job. Good candidates typically invest more time than managers preparing for the interview, reading books and getting inside information on the company. The Internet gives candidates access to more information than ever before.

We shouldn't write off the value of interviews totally. Strong candidates will have more than one position in which they are interested. Which job future superstars take is likely to depend as much on the performance of the recruiter in the interview as on the candidate's replies. It's entirely possible that the critical element in the interview isn't the candidate, but the recruiter's interview skills.

The chief reason interviews don't go well is because of poor pre-planning by the recruiter. It's so easy to justify rushing into the interview without a coherent strategy. This book, though, is about Hire Performance, a systematic approach to candidate selection that focuses on objective criteria for making good hiring decisions. It has taken ten chapters to get to the point of being ready to interview. Without proper pre-planning, recruiters over-rely on the interview as the primary ingredient for their "gut-feel" approach to selection. Good planning minimizes the stress that accompanies the face-to-face meeting. If you know what to ask, how to ask it, and why you're asking, you feel more in control as a professional recruiter.

Without a systematic and objectively based approach to hiring, you've got about as much chance recruiting a winning sales team as winning the lottery.

The Question of Turf

The first issue to confront as you plan for the interview is *where* you should interview candidates. If your office projects your values and image, meet on your turf. If you can't see your desktop for the clutter, or you operate out of an office in your home, it's best to choose a neutral site. Sometimes you may need to travel to another town or state to meet with prospective candidates. In these situations, turf issues become more complicated.

Avoid restaurant meetings if you've never met the candidate before. It's not just the cost of drinks or a meal that could prove a liability. You may know within a couple of minutes that this candidate is a complete loser, but now you're stuck until either the meal is over or you can make a graceful getaway.

Hotel lobbies work well for initial interviews. Find a comfortable location away from the main flow of traffic to avoid distractions and interruptions. If you like the candidate, suggest the interview continue over lunch.

In general, recruiters should never meet a candidate for the first time at the applicant's home or office. The social dynamic is all-wrong. You are put in the role of guest and the candidate as host. Professional interviewing requires that the interviewer be in the dominant social position. Otherwise the recruiter is less likely to be as assertive or inquisitive as the situation may demand. Similarly, the salesperson is put at a disadvantage because he or she is not able to demonstrate critical social skills required in the typical sales call where the rep meets clients on their turf.

Multiple Interview Process

Here's a true story that illustrates two very important principles:

1. The less turnover you can afford on your sales team, the more interviews with candidates you should plan.

2. Do not hire on the first interview regardless of how impressed you are or how pressured you feel to make a quick decision.

I was recruiting sales people in another city. I ran an ad in the local paper promoting an informational meeting at a downtown hotel. I flew into the city the night before, got a good night's rest, and prepared my standard presentation. The next morning I found the assigned meeting room and set up the room. With everything ready, I sat down to wait for those who would heed my recruitment ad's call to action, but no one showed. I waited for an hour. After another hour, I was about to retrieve my brochures and flipchart when, at last, one dapper looking young man poked his nose inside the door.

"Am I late?" he laughed.

"Better late than never," I said trying to keep a positive demeanor. "Come on in and let me show you what you missed?"

I had invested over $1,600 in plane tickets, hotel costs, and newspaper ads, not to mention my time. I wasn't about to leave town with nothing to show for it.

He handed me his resume and, nose lifted slightly in the air, introduced himself as "D. Thomas Smith" or some snobbish-sounding name. The way he talked, arriving late, flashy clothes, glamorous picture on the resume – I knew right away I was dealing with a major Performer whose style was probably not compatible with my own Performer-Commander tendencies.

D. Thomas did most of the talking. He told me about himself, his impressive contact list, his interests and legendary ability to sell. He was a total jerk –

everything I DIDN'T want on my team, but I was desperate to show something for the investment of my trip. I kept thinking how the VP of Sales would give me trouble if I came back with nothing to show for the trip but a stack of expense vouchers. So, I violated my multiple interview standard. And thus began the long, slippery slope.

I started selling D. Thomas on the position. I explained that he would need to complete a sales assessment.

"Oh," he said with a dismissive wave of his hand, "I don't think that will be necessary. You see, the reason I was late getting here was that I had an interview with another company (a competitor of mine) and they've already made me an offer. Now, I think I'd rather work with your organization, but I don't have time to take your 'little test.' If you can't make up your mind today, I'm really not interested."

I threw away my Hire Performance. I allowed myself to be emotionally influenced away from my strategic plan. His sales pitch wowed me. I thought if D. Thomas can sell me in the interview, he could sell iceboxes to Eskimos. I hired him on the spot.

Six weeks later I had to justify to my boss why I had abandoned my recruitment strategy to hire such a con man. The "D" in D. Thomas must have stood for "Dud." He ended up alienating one of our biggest clients and was recruiting others in my sales organization away to his next selling scheme. D. Thomas cost our company tens of thousands of dollars in wasted time and effort. It would have been far less expensive to re-run the ads and spend three or four more nights in the hotel. In fact, I could have lived like a king for several months on the road for what it cost to hire the wrong person.

Make it an inviolable rule: **never hire anyone on the first interview**. It's like dating. When you meet someone for the first time, you're on your best behavior trying to impress the candidate, and the candidate is putting his or her best foot forward to win your approval. Now, this is hardly the kind of environment in which to base a decision worth tens of thousands of dollars, not to mention reputations and careers. Have the discipline to step back from the candidates who give a great interview. Get your objectivity back. Review what you learned in the interview and how it squares with your Hire Performance strategy.

How to Have a Great First Interview

The first interview should take approximately 20-45 minutes. Here are eight steps to make it a positive, productive experience.

1. **Greet the candidate.**
   Introduce yourself as necessary, and put the candidate at ease with social chatter. Smile as you chitchat to build rapport. Make eye contact. Thank the individual for coming. Ask if he/she had any trouble finding you. Gauge the amount of preliminaries to the social skills and needs of the candidate.

   Is she comfortable and relaxed meeting you? Is she friendly or formal? Will this first impression work with your clients? What selling style behaviors immediately emerge? Performers shake hands robustly, speak forcefully, and are excessively good-natured and highly expressive. Commanders will come across more self-controlled and matter-of-fact. Analyzers will smile, not laugh (usually Analyzers don't show their teeth when they smile). Analyzers are less expressive and may appear to be slightly anxious and more formal than other types. Empathizers speak somewhat softly, smile genuinely, shake hands with less firmness, and nod their heads "yes" as you talk to them. If you suspect Commander or Analyzer tendencies, minimize the small talk and get on with the meeting. The other two types (Empathizers and Performer) are likely to go on chatting for as long as you let them.

2. **Provide a brief overview.**
   Transition to the business at hand by briefly summarizing what's going to happen in the current interview process. Analyzers need the structure, so tell them how much time you expect to take. Commanders and Performers will have already started to hijack the control of the meeting away from you by both conscious and unconscious strategies, so it's important that you regain the initiative and maintain control of the interview. The simplest way to do this is to provide a simple verbal checklist of what's going to happen in the first interview and how long it should take.

   Do not mention anything about a second interview or assessments at this stage.

3. **Ask the candidate to complete a job application.**
   Complete the application right away. Do not delay or allow the candidate to distract you from completing this step. Not only can you clarify information

that may have been omitted from the candidate's resume, but you also protect yourself legally. A resume is not a legal document. The properly prepared job application is legally binding. Misleading statements on a job application give you a legal footing if you have to dismiss the employee later.

The employment application should provide not only basic biographical information (name, address, phone) and work history, but should include statements granting permission for you to contact references, conduct credit checks or drug screens, and any other necessary investigative activity. Sample applications can be obtained from your state employment office. Your attorney can advise you on the specific appropriate language to satisfy state law and meet appropriate EEOC guidelines, if any, for your unique situation. When the candidate signs and dates the application, you have a legal document.

The candidate should complete the employment application in private. You may leave the room or interviewing area as the candidate completes the application or you may prefer to usher the job seeker to another location with instructions to bring the application to you when finished. Work out in advance how you will handle the privacy issue, particularly if you are meeting the candidate at a neutral site.

Quick-scan the application in the same way you learned to scan resumes. Look for the obvious things: neatness, completeness, gaps, and most important – is it signed and dated. If you received a resume prior to the first interview, you should be able to quickly verify any items you highlighted in yellow on the resume.

4. **Ask a general question about the candidate.**
Every job interview I've endured starts with one of two questions (sometimes both).

   1. "Tell me a little about yourself."

   2. "Where do you see yourself in five years?"

Most applicants expect these questions and are probably prepared with an answer. Starting the interview with a broad question gives the candidate a chance to get over any nervousness and adjust to the interview situation. This is not a throwaway question. Be sure you listen, as you can pick up valuable clues about the person's communication skills and selling style in these first few moments of social interaction.

Although it takes some practice, professional interviewers must listen at two levels simultaneously. Not only do you need to evaluate **what** the candidate is saying, but also *how* she/he is saying it. Listen to the content of the response. Where does she start describing herself? Does he talk about self more than relationships, education more than experience? What a person says first is a strong indication of personal priorities and values.

It's easy to get focused on the content and miss the meta-communication; that is, *how* is the candidate saying it. Does the response seem canned or rambling? Are answers coherent or not clearly thought out? Does the candidate talk too much or not enough? Can you understand him? Is her self-presentation appropriate to the product or service you sell?

At this stage never criticize either what is said or how. Give only positive feedback to the candidate's self-presentation.

5. **Describe the position briefly and tell the candidate something about the company.**
Talk about the main duties of the job. Describe the title of the person to whom the position is accountable along with a general picture of the qualifications required for the job. Here's an example: "Lee, XYZ Widgets needs a direct sales rep in our North Carolina region to service our current customers and at the same time develop new accounts to build our market share. The North Carolina rep position reports to our Eastern regional sales manager who is based in Richmond, Virginia. The skills that we've determined are critical to succeed in this position are strong communication skills, prospecting, problem solving, and at least two years of experience in direct sales."

As you speak, pay attention to how well the candidate listens. At least half of selling is listening. Does the candidate interrupt? Ask questions? Clarify? Probe? Quickly loose interest?

If, on the basis of a negative first impression, you have already made the decision not to hire the individual, use the interview as an opportunity to create positive PR for your firm and to sharpen your skills. Instead of talking about the position, you might describe the company's growth and position in the marketplace. Don't immediately dismiss an unqualified job seeker who somehow slipped through your initial screen. Treat every candidate with patience and respect. Develop habits that keep doors open. After all, you never know where you might meet again or whom the candidate knows.

6. **Ask the candidate for questions.**
Close this section of the interview by answering any final questions the candidate raises. Aggressive candidates may want immediate feedback about their performance or where they stand in relation to others you have interviewed. Be honest about strengths and guarded about sharing your impressions of weaknesses. Don't give away too much information about other candidates, salary or commission structure, or your hiring deadlines. If pressured for an answer, say you have other interviews scheduled and provide a general timeframe for reaching a decision. You may initially react negatively to candidates who pressure you, but what does this assertiveness say about the prospect's initiative?

Be wary of any candidate whose only interest in the first interview is money. There's nothing wrong with candidates wanting to know about the general pay range or inquiring about benefits, especially if you don't publish the pay structure in your recruitment ad. However, the candidate whose interest in the job is pegged only to compensation is a red flag within the Hire Performance model. Reps who are only money-motivated will be the first to leave your company for a better offer.

7. **Next steps.**
If the interview has not gone well, you will want to conclude the interview at an appropriate point. Give your well rehearsed "Don't-call-us-we'll-call-you" speech. You might explain that you have several more candidates to interview and provide the general timeframe in which the hiring decision will be made. Thank the candidate for coming and promise that you'll be in touch about any next steps should they be necessary.

Always write a thank you letter to candidates you have interviewed and turned down. That letter should affirm their skills and aptitude (after all, they did convince you to interview them) and inform them that the position for which they were applying has been filled. You may want to keep their resume on file and tell them so. Wish them well and thank them for their courtesy and professionalism.

If the first interview has gone well and the candidate matches your Hire Performance criteria, review with your prospect the next steps in your recruitment process. Explain the multiple interview process. Never mention a second interview until you know you're interested in pursuing the candidate further.

If you use a hiring test (like SalesMAP™), explain that you'll be using a selection assessment as one of several tools (along with checking references and a second interview) to help you evaluate whether the job is the right fit for the individual. Talking about the fit of the job to the person more than trying to fit the person to the job, not only affirms the candidate, but it also builds positive professional regard in both interviewee and interviewer.

If you want your candidate to complete the selection test at home, give the prospect a test booklet and answer sheet to take with them. Review the instructions briefly and tell your candidate how and when to get the results to your for scoring.

If the assessment is not to be taken home, it's best if you can arrange, if at all possible, for the candidate to complete the questionnaire at the end of your first interview. Should this be inconvenient for your candidate, arrange a time the assessment can be completed. The candidate should complete any profile in private.

8. **Schedule your next interview.**
   If you are using an assessment, explain that you'll have the results in advance of your next interview. You'll need a ready-made answer if the candidate asks about receiving a copy of the test results. Your policy about giving out assessment results will depend a lot upon the assessment you use. General assessments (such as personality or temperament profiles) have more potential for misunderstanding and mischief than highly targeted ones (core competency tests). This is because general tests are more subjective and can be discriminatory if they present a picture of the way somebody "is." Skill assessments tend to be more objective and less threatening to the candidate. My general rule of thumb is that I do NOT share test results reports, but rather will interpret results in general terms. You'll develop these skills in the next chapter.

Schedule 60 to 90 minutes for the next interview.

Conclusion

First interviews should be brief, general, information-gathering events conducted on your turf. You're trying to determine the kind of first impression this candidate is likely to make with your customers. You also need to generate a legal employment application and, if you use an assessment, work it in as early into the interview process as possible. Although interviews are only marginally effective in uncovering sales talent, a well-planned, professional first interview can be a positive first step in building a winning sales team.

Chapter 12

Using Sales Hiring Tests

Primers are the most basic introductory texts on a subject. This chapter is a primer on choosing and using hiring tests in your efforts to recruit a winning sales team.

Traditionally, recruiters have plugged sales assessments into the hiring process after a successful first interview. By this time the interviewer had formed a positive opinion about the job seeker and wanted to validate their gut feel with some objective information. Hiring tests given *after* an initial interview are called "post-screens."

But today's technology is drastically changing not only how hiring tests are given, but when and why as well. In the days of paper-pencil tests, recruiters had to meet with candidates face-to-face first before giving them the test. Today, hiring tools are available 24/7/365 anywhere in the world via the Internet. Web-based, paperless selection assessments allow recruiters to *pre-screen* candidates; that is, managers may send candidates to an internet site to complete a hiring profile and receive results *before* the first interview.

Pre-screening is much more cost efficient for recruiters than old-fashioned post-screening. Pre-screens don't require sales managers to lose time talking to people who don't meet their basic profile. Recruiters gain a huge advantage by having objective information before the first meeting, so they can use the first interview to zero in on specific productivity issues. Pre-screening can easily reduce by half the amount of time needed for interviewing.

Five Objections to Using Hiring Tests

In this chapter, you'll learn about two basic kinds of sales hiring tests and why one in particular will increase your Hire Performance. But first, we need to address the basic question of why someone should use any sales selection assessment. In spite of their popularity, some recruiters refuse or hesitate to use sales hiring tests. Here are answers to the top five objections.

Objection #5 – "I don't need it."

Every recruiter uses some type of selection test. Selection tests aren't necessarily limited to a page of multiple-choice questions.

Take, for example, the selection test used by retail giant, John Cash Penney. His recruitment strategy included taking potential managers to lunch or dinner. Not only would he learn a great deal about their social poise, but J. C. Penney was also convinced he could discern important qualities of their potential management style. During the meal, Penney watched to see if the candidate seasoned food before tasting it. He thought anyone too quick with salt and pepper might also be too impetuous for Penney's more cautious style.

J.C. Penney's hiring test might not satisfy EEOC standards today, but his methodology illustrates how veteran recruiters and managers develop, over a career of hiring decisions, informal indicators of talent. Experience leads them to trust some marker behaviors. The question is *not* do recruiters use hiring assessments. The real issue is whether the hiring assessments used by recruiters are subjective or objective, validated or purely fanciful?

One recruiter who, for obvious reasons, shall remain nameless, says he never hires anyone with a beard or mustache. "Never had a one that worked out," he said. That's his selection test! He is convinced facial hair predicts productivity!

What about you? Do you have informal selection criteria? Your personal style will predispose you to the informal measurements you use to test and categorize prospects. Performers evaluate candidates by personal appearance or the kind of car the applicant drives. Empathizers judge on the basis of eye contact or quickness at building rapport. Commanders assess candidates on the basis of the prospect's decisiveness and self-confidence. Candidates with a good vocabulary impress Analyzers. We know that good producers are a balance of all these attributes. Consequently, recruiters with balanced Life-Needs are most likely to use informal assessments to best advantage.

The formal sales selection tests are designed to deliver validated factual information. You can't rely always on "gut feel." While every recruiter develops professional sensitivities, it is important to be clear about the criteria used to evaluate sales candidates. Recruiters who say they don't need selection tests are often intuitive, information-avoidant amateurs who are either too impatient to learn how to use a selection tool or vain enough to believe they are God's gift to staffing.

Objection #4 – "I don't believe sales tests can predict success."
To be honest, this objection seldom gets expressed exactly this way. More often it surfaces as, "*I used such-and-so Sales Success Test and it didn't really help.*"

Not all sales tests are equally helpful. Some are a complete waste. Sometimes an assessment doesn't work because it's built on faulty theory. In the early 1900's you might have invested in a phrenometer to help you recruit salespeople. Dubbed the product of the latest in scientific research, this device measured the contours of a person's head. The size and placement of cranial contusions, it was thought, held the secret to predicting success.

Studies done in the 20's said salespeople were out-going, talkative, money motivated, and driven. Arthur Miller's Willie Loman became the stereotype of the direct sales rep. Beginning in the 1950's, personality assessments became the accepted standard for assessing career productivity.

Unfortunately, by the end of the 20th century, no scientifically verifiable links could be established between personality variables and sales productivity. None. Nada. Zilch. You might as well use a phrenometer or birth order theories or temperament analysis or left-brain / right-brain typologies. None are much more predictive than a coin toss.

Tests can and do accurately measure all kinds of wonderful and interesting things. But if there's no proven correlation between what a test measures and one's ability to sell, it's as useless as a swizzle stick to a teetotaler.

SalesMAP™ is not a personality test. It measures behaviors; specifically, behaviors that help or hinder contact initiation. SalesMAP™ does a lousy job of predicting success in sales organizations where salespeople do not initiate contact with prospective buyers or current clients. But in organizations where prospecting and client contact are important aspects of sales success (which our research indicates is the most critical behavior to sales success in direct sales), SalesMAP™ is a highly accurate tool to help forecast productivity.

Before you use any sales selection assessment, you must have evidence that what a test measures is directly linked with sales productivity.

Objection #3 – "Tests are hard to understand. I don't want to become an amateur psychologist."

Every manager is a psychologist, whether he or she wants to be or not. Ultimately, managing is a people business and psychology is the study of why people behave the way they do. If you're good with people, you stand a better chance of being a good manager and recruiter.

It's true – tests can be hard to understand. In fact, some assessments are intentionally complicated. Users are required to attend certification programs before they can purchase or use some tests. Marketing considerations more than intellectual necessity usually drive this strategy. Why merely sell a test when you can up-sell a whole catalog of products and services, all designed to help you better interpret the test. Now, that's a racket!

Some tests are hard to understand because human behavior itself is so fickle and full of vagaries. Any test designer will tell you it's a challenge to have a test that is both scientifically precise and user friendly. The first version of SalesMAP™ was huge and complicated. Preliminary statistical analysis proved very promising. The scientists and statisticians loved it. Unfortunately, sales managers couldn't understand it. So, it was back to the drawing board again and again to synthesize scientific reliability with real-world practicality.

Objection #2 – "Tests are too expensive and just add to the cost of hiring."

This objection is being heard less and less from sales organizations as the cost of hiring a sales flop escalates well into six figures. Testing candidates for a sales position can save you money in three significant ways.

1. **Sales tests can save you the cost of a bad hire.**
   In one recent research study of more than 20 companies, hiring a sales dud now costs the average company about $25,000. Based on this study, using SalesMAP™ as a hiring tool would have improved sales productivity in the sample by 45% overall and saved $273,450.00 in bad hiring costs, making the average SalesMAP™ assessment worth $5,411.76. That represents an average return on investment (ROI) of 4832%.

   A validated sales selection test like SalesMAP™ is worth literally ten times its weight in gold for the typical direct sales organization.

   Here's a simple rule for weighing the value of a sales hiring assessment. Figure the cost of a sales hiring mistake, including lost opportunity (the money you would have made if you had hired a good salesperson). If you can pay less than 2% of your bad hire cost for a selection test, it's a bargain. Consider it an insurance premium to indemnify you against the loss of bringing a sales dud on board.

2. **Sales tests can drive down the cost of training.**
   Hiring right in the first place means your training programs can be informational rather than transformational. Transformational training is the most expensive kind. Transformational training requires that you gauge your curriculum to the lowest common denominator of sales inexperience and run everybody through the same cookie-cutter program. In most cases, you end up wasting valuable time and resources trying to *transform* civilians into a sales force. Informational training, on the other hand, is targeted to the specific needs of each recruit. This individual approach is not only faster and more cost efficient, but it promotes increased morale, because informational training is less likely to alienate or frustrate sales veterans. Experienced reps new to a company may only need product knowledge, information about administrative details, and perhaps a little remedial training in unique skills necessary to your marketing approach.

   Speaking of veterans, testing can lower training costs by giving you a clearer picture of the veteran salesperson's skill-level and personal issues. Just because someone has experience in your industry doesn't mean it was *good* experience. She may have learned bad habits that will impair her ability to be productive in your organization. She may have developed a blind spot to issues critical to success with your clients. Assessments, coupled with follow-up interviews, can provide extremely helpful information for developing career reps.

3. Sales tests can help reduce turnover.
Hiring the right people not only impacts the bottom line by hiring better salespeople and lowering training costs, it also contributes to higher team morale and lower turnover rates. People who fit well with the organization and sell a lot are happier and tend to hang around longer than employees whose style doesn't match the team or selling environment. Good salespeople want to sell, not sit through hours of indoctrination or remedial training. Testing allows you to identify people with selling skill-sets already in place. The reps who can get up and running rapidly not only help you recover your recruitment costs more quickly, but they improve profitability by taking less time and energy managing emotional and productivity issues.

Another way sales assessments reduce turnover and save money involves team dynamics and selling style. Some sales assessments identify the kind of manager that will most likely work best with the candidate. For example, let's say your assessment diagnoses that your new salesperson is somebody who needs to be in control of his own time and doesn't work as well on a team as on his own. Assigning such an individual to a "touchy-feely" manager is a prescription for disaster. Some reps will develop beautifully in a customer-oriented consultative sales approach. They will begin to progress almost instantaneously while others will want to close sales quickly. Geeks need to sell technical stuff and can become unglued when they don't get facts and figures. Conversely, put a prima donna Performer under the supervision of a bean-counter manager and eventually one or the other is out the door.

Testing can help you spot these potential teamwork issues and provide valuable intelligence for assigning the right kind of rep to the right type of manager. It's important to match the needs and skills of people to the right sales and management environment.

Objection #1 – "I'm worried about the liability of giving selection tests."

It's a sign of the times. J.C. Penney didn't worry about government guidelines for hiring and firing. But today legal issues have become the number one concern among HR professionals and sales recruiters. Liability issues are more top-of-mind for potential test-users than cost or need. As overburdened as business owners and managers feel with government regulations and requirements, U.S. law is still relatively lenient compared to legal requirements in Europe, Australia or New Zealand where it usually takes a full year or longer for companies to document a dismissal for any reason.

Managers and recruiters frequently ask, "How do I know if the assessment I use is approved by the EEOC?" There are no government-approved selection tests. The EEOC does not endorse any test. The law requires that selection tests must do two simple things:

- They must measure something critical to job performance.

- They must not discriminate on any grounds other than variables associated with job performance.

Hiring tests are, by definition, discriminatory; that is, they classify individuals according to some variable. As long as recruiters can document that the discriminating variable being assessed is critical to job performance, Hire Performers have nothing to fear from government regulators.

Tom, for instance, was a sales recruiter from a small manufacturing company. He used a well-known sales personality test to screen candidates, but was also interested in SalesMAP.

"We've been using this assessment for years," Tom said. "Why should I use SalesMAP? Aren't all these hiring tests the same?"

I asked Tom if I could look at the job description for the position he was trying to fill. I'm not a lawyer, but it only took a second or two to see that Tom's company could be legally vulnerable.

"What does that personality test tell you about your candidates?" I asked Tom. "What are you looking for?"

"Drive, determination, somebody really out-going – the usual stuff," he replied.

"Where is that stuff in your job description?" I asked, handing him the job description.

It wasn't there. His job description was list of behaviors – what Tom expected salespeople to do, not what they should be. The salesperson that sold Tom the personality test claimed drive, determination, and extroversion were important for salespeople. Tom couldn't disagree, but without specifically stating that these attributes were required, any applicant turned down on the basis of the profile could sue Tom's company and likely win.

All the parts of Hire Performance work together synergistically. When approached strategically, the ad will work with the assessment; the assessment will dovetail with the interview, and the interview with motivational strategy. Each contributes to the other and reinforces the goal of recruiting a winning sales team.

But even if Tom includes those psychological buzzwords in the job description, the company is still exposed. All that is required is for some troublemaker to make Tom produce his turnover statistics and ask for the reasons of dismissal. Since everybody took the same hiring profile, it's obvious that a lot of people who tested high in drive, determination, or extroversion turned out to be job failures. Tom was inferring a connection between production and personality that just isn't there. And quick as a flash your attorney is whispering in your ear, "We'd better settle."

When I was first designing SalesMAP™, I remember one manager who had grown cynical about using selection assessments. "If these tests are so #@&%$ good at predicting behavior," he growled, "why can't they spot the people who are most likely to sue me if they don't like the results?"

At first I dismissed the objection as just one more manager having a bad day. But the more I thought about it, the more sense this began to make. I came up with something I called Validity Check.

The SalesMAP Validity Check scale actually has nothing to do with statistical validity. It is designed to provoke and measure behaviors that indicate the test-taker may not be open to getting objective feedback about results. Not everyone who takes a hiring test is happy about it. SalesMAP detects and measures this attitude toward taking the assessment. If the test-taker gets more and more provoked as they complete the questionnaire, the Validity Check score drops. When it reaches a certain point, it tells the defensive test-taker to ignore the results because the data is unreliable. Are the scores really unreliable? Not at all.

The assessment has a built-in safeguard to help reduce the risk of someone becoming upset by test results and taking it out on you or your sales organization.

Two Kinds of Tests

Sales hiring tests can be divided into two general classifications: sales personality tests and behavioral profiles.

Sales personality tests are the most popular type of sales assessment. They've been around a long time. Sales personality tests attempt to measure the psychological makeup of the individual, peering deep inside the candidate's character and in-born traits. The assumption behind personality profiling is that it takes a certain kind of person to succeed in sales; a person usually described with words like "extroverted," "social," "out-going," someone possessing "ego strength" and "drive." Sales psychology tests assume that if someone possesses the "right stuff" she will be comfortable meeting people and promoting the company's product or service.

Identifying a sales personality test can be difficult because the assessment may not use the word "personality" in its title or description. Sometimes they're called temperament or preference profiles. One easy way to spot a sales personality assessment is to look for questions that ask individuals to describe themselves using lists of adjectives (descriptive words). For example, a sales personality questionnaire would be filled with items like this:

Which of the following is most like you?

A. Exciting

B. Analytical

C. Careful

D. Creative

Many sales personality tests will ask questions that have nothing to do with selling. One of my favorites is:

I like to put my hand in warm, squishy mud.

True   False

Another way to identify a sales personality assessment is to read the small print that says, "Not to be used for selection purposes without proper validation." Reputable sales personality tests contain disclaimers about their reliability in the hiring process. If you don't see this warning language, check out the validation material provided by the test manufacturer. Be suspicious of any test claiming validity based only on "test-retest reliability" or "inter-item correlations." These measures do not mean the test will predict anything. Sales personality tests may accurately pigeonhole someone as a certain type of individual, but there's no evidence that personality variables universally make better salespeople. Just because someone can sell doesn't mean they will sell.

The second type of sales hiring test measures behaviors. Sometimes called core competency profiles, they attempt to measure the basic skills necessary for the job. You can identify a behavior profile by looking for questions that focus on what the salesperson does rather than what the salesperson is. Look for scenarios like this:

You are on your way to a sales appointment and discover a serious typographical error in your presentation. What are you most likely to do (what have you done in the most recent past)?

A. Call the client and re-schedule.

B. Scratch out the error and apologize to the client for the error.

C. Give the presentation and hope the customer doesn't notice the error.

D. I don't know what I'd do in this situation.

Behavior profiles originated in the 1980's and are growing in popularity. They can be more easily validated since behavior is objective and measurable rather than subjective and esoteric (like personality variables).

As you might guess from the reliance of this book on the SalesMAP core competency profile, Hire Performance mandates behavioral profiling as far superior to personality profiling if your goal is to recruit a winning sales team.

Why You Should Never Use a Sales Personality Test to Screen Sales Candidates

Because selling is a behavior, you should only use hiring tests (such as SalesMAP™) that measure sales behaviors. Avoid "sales personality" tests like the plague. Here are five business reasons why.

Reason #1 – Sales personality tests are easily manipulated by the very people they indicate you should hire.
This is a curious phenomenon. Few sales personality profiles detect, let alone measure test manipulation behavior. Sales personality tests assume everyone taking a hiring assessment tells "the truth, the whole truth, and nothing but the truth." In fact, about 40% of salespeople exaggerate, second-guess, or deliberately sabotage selection assessments. Rather than discount manipulated results, sales personality tests actually declare these are the people who have "ego strength" or "a persuasive personality" – necessary requirements, they say, for good salespeople.

OK, let's think about this for a minute. Why accept exaggeration as a virtue in your assessment when you wouldn't accept it on a resume?

If a test recommends those who most easily manipulate results, you don't know what you're hiring! If your candidate will manipulate your hiring test to make a good impression, why wouldn't the same person, now your new employee, manipulate call reports or customers or make exaggerated claims for your product or service?

Hire Performance demands an assessment that detects test-taking behavior and uses information about how the person took the test to evaluate the quality of responses. Without such measurements, the only picture recruiters get is the glowing portrait a test-savvy candidate can paint of himself.

Reason #2 – Sales personality tests discriminate on the basis of what people ARE.
When hiring someone, it's illegal to discriminate on the basis of race, sex, or other inborn attributes. Yet every day, sales organizations think nothing about giving sales personality profiles built on the premise that great salespeople are BORN that way.

Although one's personality may change somewhat over time, personality is generally regarded as a stable trait. You can't change the fact that you're an introvert or an extrovert any more than you can change your race or sexual preference (and if you could change these things, it wouldn't be cost effective for the typical business enterprise). Sales personality profiling can and does have serious legal implications in today's litigious workplace.

Speaking in broad terms, all recruiting is discriminatory; that is, you choose some and reject others. Hire Performance demands an assessment that discriminates on the basis of behaviors – what people DO, not the way they ARE.

Reason #3 – Sales personality tests have little, if any, basis in research.
Study after study fails to prove any correlation between personality and sales production. There simply is no single "sales personality." In spite of all the fancy names, most sales personality tests measure only two variables: "extroversion" (socially out-going) and, to a lesser extent, what psychologists call "neurosis" (anxiety, risk sensitivity). Fifty years ago it was probably true that out-going risk-takers were likely to sell better than shy doomsayers, especially in commission-only direct sales. But in the hotly competitive global marketplace of the 21st century, sales organizations need the strengths of risk-averse analytical types to grow incremental sales as well as provide strategic customer service. Highly extroverted, driven reps that might do well at small dollar, short-term sales completely undermine high value sales.

At best, sales personality tests might tell you if your candidate CAN sell. There are undoubtedly aptitudes and social skills that more closely match the preferences of your clientele and marketing approach. However, personality tests make one huge *assumption* – if someone can sell, he/she *will* sell. There is no basis for this inference in research or practice. One of the most shocking stats I share in our prospecting workshops is that the average US direct sales rep is only working at about 37% of his or her perceived capacity. They all can sell, but their behavior doesn't match their ability.

Sales managers tell me this is their greatest frustration: recruiting people who have all the skills and talent to be a great rep, but who don't perform anywhere near their potential.

Hire Performance demands an assessment that will measure not only if a candidate CAN sell, but also whether the person WILL do what it takes to generate sales.

Reason #4 – Sales personality tests are designed to tell you what you expect.
It's the stuff of horoscopes and psychics. They "work" by making general statements about vaguely defined concepts that fit the experience of most people. Here's an example. Suppose I said to you, "You had some difficulty with your sexual development in your teenage years," I'd probably be right on the money, wouldn't I? Well, it's not because I'm so smart, it's merely due to the fact that I know the odds are extremely high that this statement applies to almost everyone. It's the same with sales personality assessments. These test results are filled with similarly universal statements.

Now here's where it gets really interesting. The more money paid for a sales personality assessment, the higher its perceived accuracy rate. It's not unusual for recruiters to report 90% success ratios using tests that measure ego, drive, and whether someone is a "hunter" or a "farmer." What's going on here?

Most sales personality profiles are given after the recruiter has already screened the candidate. They need a post-screen to provide "objective" feedback confirming or denying impressions from the initial interview. Developers of sales psychology tests know that the majority of recruiters are extroverts who don't pay a lot of attention to details and don't like to be criticized or told they're wrong about anything, particularly AFTER they've made a decision.

Psychologists call this *the law of cognitive dissonance*. Simply put, it states that once you've committed to something, the more your perception will shift to confirm your preconceived choice.

Jane Recruiter has already formed the opinion that Candidate A would be a good salesperson. She invites Mr. A to a second interview and wants him to take a $150 sales personality test. Jane has now reinforced her opinion by her willingness to invest money and her professional reputation in Mr. A. Cognitive dissonance means Jane will non-consciously avoid or distrust any input that questions her choice. Jane's not stupid. It's just the way her brain works. Because most sales personality tests measure the obvious (extroversion and neurosis), they quite easily confirm Jane's preconceived ideas. In those extreme cases where Jane has completely misjudged a candidate, Jane will question the validity of the assessment and complain that the profile is wrong.

Hire Performance demands an assessment that measures what is not always obvious and dares to tell the truth.

Reason #5 – You can easily disprove the validity of sales personality tests. Answering this one basic question easily exposes the weakness of using sales personality assessments to recruit a winning sales team:

How many reps that didn't work out failed because of personality issues?

In a recent survey of the causes of sales turnover, only 7% of managers said turnover was the result of any personality issue (conflict with a manager or team member, shyness, lack of sociability, etc). Approximately 70% of failures were attributed to poor production. They failed because they didn't sell enough.

Remember – the core competency of all sales activity is contact initiation. What good is it if someone is "out-going" and "dynamic" or possesses a great deal of "ego strength" if the rep doesn't get in front of customers and prospects! Just because someone can sell does not mean they will sell. Hire Performance demands an assessment that will measure key behavior variables proven to be correlated with success in sales.

Conclusion

Be a smart consumer of sales selection tests. Look at the kinds of questions asked. Request validation information, not just client lists.

Behavioral assessments are better than sales psychology tests if they detect exaggeration and other manipulations, ask questions about what candidates do in client contact situations (rather than what candidates are), and have the integrity and courage to be something more than a recruitment horoscope.

Chapter 13

Follow-up Interviews & Behavioral Interviewing Skills

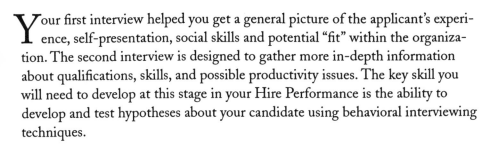

Your first interview helped you get a general picture of the applicant's experience, self-presentation, social skills and potential "fit" within the organization. The second interview is designed to gather more in-depth information about qualifications, skills, and possible productivity issues. The key skill you will need to develop at this stage in your Hire Performance is the ability to develop and test hypotheses about your candidate using behavioral interviewing techniques.

Before the Second Interview

Before the second interview you should have already completed these critical action items:

1. Completed all background and reference checks.

2. Scored, printed, and reviewed your selection assessment results (if used).

3. Formulated your hypotheses and behavioral interview questions.

Let's look at each in more detail.

1. **Complete all background and reference checks.**
   Run a credit check. Good credit indicates integrity. Bad credit, slow-pays, and judgments may point to someone who not only does not take commitments seriously, but who may also be pressured to take short-cuts or be less than honest with customers and you. Desperate people seldom turn out to be top producers.

Be sure your employment application grants you permission to obtain this background information. Consult with an attorney on the legal language appropriate to your state.

Run a motor vehicle report. Checking your candidate's driving record should be a standard procedure for any serious candidate whether or not the applicant will be on selling on the road. A good driving record usually indicates someone who is prudent and responsible. Numerous tickets and accidents should be a red flag that an individual may enjoy taking unnecessary risks or disrespects authority.

Verify employment. Although, as discussed earlier, previous employers are not likely to share much meaningful information, verifying employment dates can uncover gaps that may have gone unreported in the candidate's resume or application. It's better to find out missing information before you hire the slick-talking candidate. Gaps in the employment history are more critical in older applicants than candidates just out of school. If you notice a gap, ask the candidate about it. Many times applicants try to hide employers from which they were fired or with whom they did not get along. Try to reassure your candidate you only need to verify dates of employment. Ask if there were any problems, then listen carefully. Does the explanation sound reasonable or fanciful? If you suspect the candidate is still being less than honest about the disparity, you'll want to terminate the interview as soon as possible. Do not pressure candidates to reveal what they are covering up. It's enough to know that anyone who is less than candid in a job interview is not likely to improve his or her reliability as time goes on.

If degrees or certifications are necessary for the position, get transcripts. Ask for photocopies of certificates for certification programs.

Request income tax returns. If the salary history you requested seems too good to be true, ask to see copies of the individual's income tax returns. Although not every candidate who hesitates or even refuses to comply with this request is necessarily guilty of misrepresentation, you will introduce an element of accountability into the relationship early on that will ward off dishonest candidates and protect you.

2. **Score, print, and review your selection assessment results (if used).**

    Review test returns for strengths and challenges. What are the positives and negatives the assessment identifies? Do they correspond to your review of the resume? Get out the colored markers you used to highlight the candidate's resume and use the same color scheme to review test results.

    Always compliment before criticizing. This is an important Hire Performance technique to learn. Never voice a concern or ask a potentially difficult question that you don't precede with a strength you've found in the candidate's skills and qualifications. This interview skill minimizes defensive reactions and helps candidates feel more at ease with you, especially if you use a selection assessment. Since you don't want to be fumbling for a compliment during the interview, you should jot down some compliments next to the areas of concern on the assessment report or the in the margins of the resume.

    Decide ahead of time whether to share assessment results. Should you or shouldn't you share the results of hiring tests with candidates? There's no single right answer to this question. It depends on the amount of time you have to spend in the interview process; and the nature of the results.

    If you have adequate time and the candidate has positive test results, use the interview time to build a strong bond between you and the applicant. Top producers are always open to learning anything about themselves that will improve their productivity. Potential superstars will appreciate your taking time to give them professional feedback. It demonstrates a powerful commitment on your part to develop their sales potential.

    Poor results should probably not be shared with test-takers. You're not running a testing service. If a candidate wants to know about test outcomes, quickly summarize one or two strengths and move on with the interview. Never identify performance issues as revealed by any test. Make it clear that tests don't hire, you do. Abdicating your hiring responsibility to a test could leave you open to legal hassles if the test you give is not properly validated. Selection assessments supplement Hire Performance and are not a substitute for recruiter responsibility.

If you review test results, show the candidate your profile first. Your choice to be self-revealing will greatly diminish any sense of threat and build a powerful bond between you and the candidate. The candidate may be challenged in a way with which you are familiar. Rather than being threatened by this information, you can use assessment insights proactively to underscore your commitment to be a sales coach, and not merely a babysitter.

Some recruiters are uncertain how to introduce assessment results into the interview. One simple approach is to ask the candidate, "How did you feel taking that Survey?" Listen carefully to the emotion behind the words as the applicant responds. Is he apprehensive? Is she curious? Did he feel threatened? Is she open to learning anything she can about herself? Is this salesperson coachable? What does the reaction to the assessment say about emotional maturity?

Next, mirror their response. Mirroring means you embody the feelings behind the words as well as what they say. For example, you could respond, "You know, I had some of those same feelings when I first took that test. Here's what it said about me." At this point, show the candidate your assessment results. Without revealing the candidate's profile, talk about something in common between your two profiles, even if it's a negative. You want to put the candidate at ease and model by your own openness the appropriate behavior for the candidate.

Summarize key findings. Depending on the overall quality of the candidate, highlight one or two of the main issues. If you are using the SalesMAP™ Hiring Report, the top three issues will be identified for you along with behavioral interview questions to ask based on the findings.

Let the candidate talk about the results. What findings are acceptable? What results seem to cause questions or concern? It's important that you not become defensive about having given the assessment or reporting its conclusions. The purpose of the test is not to label or categorize people, but to encourage candidates to talk with managers about issues important to sales productivity.

Take a break. Immediately after concluding your review of results, excuse yourself from the room. Go the restroom, get a cup of coffee, go talk with your secretary – anything to give the candidate a few moments to integrate the information you shared. Additionally, the break provides space and time to distance yourself from the role of coach and re-establish your role as interviewer with the candidate.

3. Formulate hypotheses and behavioral questions

Formulating hypotheses doesn't have to be complicated or difficult. You don't need formulas or special skills. You know the ingredients of Hire Performance. As you read their resume, review assessment results and talk with candidates, and be alert to clues that relate to sales productivity. If John's record from the department of motor vehicles is as long as your arm, your hypothesis will probably be that John is reckless and needs a lot of stimulation. If Lucy shakes hands limply and talks softly, your hypothesis may be that she may have trouble initiating contact and assertively closing sales.

The focus of this book and its approach to recruiting has been behavioral rather than psychological. That is, research demonstrates that success in selling is based not on mental states, but observable, measurable behaviors that promote productivity. In the second interview you must formulate questions that will allow you to test your hypotheses.

Formulating Behavioral Interview Questions

Behavioral interviewing is a method of asking objective, behaviorally relevant questions about past performance in order to help recruiters predict future behavior. Behavioral interviewing is a skill, which, if practiced carefully and methodically, should help you avoid the three most dangerous and counterproductive interview questions:

1. illegal questions;

2. hypothetical questions;

3. feeling-oriented questions.

1. Illegal Questions

Here are some illegal questions to avoid and permissible alternatives that you may ask in the hiring situation.

Questions about national citizenship or ethnic origin

Illegal "Are you an American citizen?"

Legal "Are you authorized to work in the United States?"

Questions about age

Illegal "How old are you?"
"When did you graduate from high school (or college)?"
"What is your birth date?"

Legal "Are you over 18 years of age?"
"What languages do you read or write?"
(This is legal only if being bilingual is critical to performing the job.)

Questions about marital or family status

Illegal "Are you married?"
"With whom do you reside?"
"Do you plan to have a family?"
"How many children do you have?"
"What are your childcare arrangements?"

Legal "Are you willing to relocate if necessary?"
"Are you free to travel?"
"The work requires considerable overtime. Can you work overtime as needed?"

NOTE: (These questions are legal *only* if asked of ALL candidates being considered for the position.)

Personal questions

Illegal "How much do you weigh?"
"How tall are you?"
"When was the date of your last physical?"

Legal "Are you able to lift 50 pounds and carry it 100 feet, as this is critical to the job?"

NOTE: These questions are legal only if asked of ALL candidates being considered for the position.

Questions about disabilities

Illegal "Do you have any disabilities?"
Asking about details of any obvious disability ("How did you lose your arm?")

Legal "Are you able to perform the physical duties of this job?"

NOTE: This question is legal only if asked after describing the physical requirements of the job and if asked equally of ALL candidates being considered for the position.

Questions about criminal background

Illegal "Have you ever been arrested?"

Legal "Have you ever been arrested for _____?"

NOTE: This question is legal only if asked about a crime reasonably related to the job and if asked equally of ALL candidates being considered for the position.

It is against U.S. law to ask any questions about religion, race or ethnic background, national origin, gender, age, marital or family status, sexual orientation, physical disability, arrests, or financial status. Best rule of thumb – when in doubt, don't ask. If a candidate volunteers any prohibited information, inform the candidate that you appreciate their openness, but you will not make any hiring decision on any basis other than the skills and qualifications of candidates.

2. Hypothetical questions

Hypothetical questions are not illegal, but they are counterproductive because they don't reveal anything except the candidate's creative abilities.

Avoid asking "What if …" questions. One of the most common mistakes made by recruiters is using hypothetical scenario questions. For example, asking, "How would you handle this or that situation?" is not a good behavioral interviewing question. Behavioral interviewing roots a question to a specific point in time. Ask, "Tell me about a time you did such and so," or, "On your last job, how did you handle this situation?"

The best recruiters invariably say that the best predictor of future performance is past performance. If a candidate has not faced the situation you describe, you are more likely to find out the truth by asking behavioral questions than hypothetical ones.

3. Feeling-Oriented Questions
Any question that begins "How do you feel about ..." moves you in the wrong direction if your goal is to build a winning sales team. Hire Performance is fact-driven, not feeling oriented. You're not hiring the candidate to feel anything, but to do something. Just because a candidate reports certain feelings toward a subject doesn't necessarily mean your rep will behave in ways consistent with those feelings. Feelings are fleeting and transitory. Behavior is objective.

Hire Performance Behavioral Interviewing Guide

The second interview must uncover and addresses potential and actual problem areas in your candidate's background and present situations that could impact productivity. But what do you ask? This section takes the guesswork out of constructing a great interview. Here are the issues you need to explore in order of their impact on productivity. (Of course, if you use SalesMAP™ these questions are provided for you in the Sales Hiring Report.).

For each behavior, I'll suggest some behavioral interview questions, and outline how you might interpret candidate responses.

Poor Sales Identity_____

Definition: Sales Identity is the degree of pride one takes in being a salesperson. People with low Sales Identity are quick to believe negative stereotypes about salespeople. Reps that spend lots of money on motivational tapes and books may have an addiction to "feel good" solutions that momentarily counteract these negative feelings. Over half of salespeople with poor Sales Identity are not even aware of this career-threatening condition.

How To Spot The Problem:

With SalesMAP™: A Sales Identity score below 50.

Without SalesMAP™: Examine your candidate's resume. Look at the job titles previously held. If a previous employer referred to a sales position as "Account Manager," "Relationship Consultant," or some other swapped-out sales identity, you'll want to be sure the rep didn't come away from the job with a negative Sales Identity. Ask these questions.

Question: *(If resume shows other titles for the sales function)*

"I see at your last job you were called ... (fill in the title). Was this a sales job? Why did the company use another term for "salesperson"?

Interpretation:
1. Does your candidate talk about avoiding the negative stereotypes associated with salespeople? If so, assume your candidate may have some residual Sales Identity issues.

2. Does the candidate explain that the title helped salespeople sell more or in some other way improved initiative, or was the designation used as an excuse or apology?

3. Watch body language and listen for any negative image of salespeople.

Question: *"What do you need in a sales manager? How important is it for a sales manager to help salespeople feel good about what they do?"*

Interpretation:
1. Does the candidate say it's important for managers to help salespeople feel good about being in sales? If so, this could indicate a negative view toward selling or someone not able to accept responsibility for the choice of a sales career.
2. What behaviors does the candidate say are necessary management behaviors? Are manager behaviors accountability-oriented (coach top performance) or motivation-oriented (keep the rep feeling good)? Motivational themes may indicate poor Sales Identity (particularly if combined with poor Sales Initiative).
3. Do you hear an over-reliance on clichés and motivational responses that provide shallow and superficial answers to complex problems?
4. Watch body language and listen for a negative image of salespeople.

Out of balance Risk Sensitivity

Definition: Risk Sensitivity is the degree to which an individual is comfortable taking calculated risks. Salespeople need a balanced Risk Sensitivity – too little and a rep could take unnecessary risks and not do "due diligence," too much and your candidate may be paralyzed by worry about worst-case scenarios. People with high Risk Sensitivity will have difficulty selling any product or service that involves risk to the consumer. These worry warts do not manage stress well and are easily overwhelmed with deadlines and pressure. Research shows that high Risk Sensitivity is catastrophic to sales productivity in direct sales organizations. Low Risk Sensitivity cannot be tolerated in sales organizations that are highly regulated or require a great deal of care or precision (technical sales, pharmaceutical sales, etc.).

How To Spot The Problem:

With SalesMAP™: A Risk Sensitivity score below 30 (low Risk Sensitivity means one is prone to take unnecessary risks) or above 70 (high Risk Sensitivity means an inclination to worry and not work well with stress).

Without SalesMAP™: Hobbies are frequently a reliable behavioral clue to Risk Sensitivity. If hobbies are not included on the resume, ask about them in the interview. Low Risk Sensitivity individuals tend to have pastimes that involve some risk, such as mountain climbing, scuba or skydiving, or active sports. High Risk Sensitivity candidates are likely to have hobbies that soothe and calm, such as reading, collecting, or other passive interests. Another clue to potential Risk Sensitivity issues may be found in the candidate's previous jobs or educational background. Education or experience as an accountant, bookkeeper, financial analyst, or corporate "gatekeeper" usually indicates low Risk Sensitivity. Additionally, because low Risk Sensitivity individuals tend to be uncomfortable in social situations, they may appear unusually nervous in the interview.

Question: *"Tell me about a time in your career when you faced a crisis? What did you do to weather it?"*

Interpretation:
1. Is the candidate quick or slow to respond? Does the candidate's description of crisis seem appropriate?
2. Low Risk Sensitive candidates may have difficulty remembering a single instance. High Risk Sensitive candidates may have difficulty limiting their answer to one instance.
3. Watch body language and listen for signals of someone who doesn't work well under pressure or who may take unnecessary risks.

Question:	*"This job can become highly stressful at times. What are some specific ways you've learned to manage stress?"*
Interpretation:	1. Is the candidate quick or slow to respond? Is the applicant able to describe a stress management strategy? High Risk Sensitive individuals become uncomfortable talking about the subject.
	2. Low Risk Sensitive candidates (risk takers) are more likely to discount stress problems. They say they work best under pressure. High Risk Sensitivity candidates could have a detailed answer as they experience stress quite frequently.
	3. Watch body language and listen for signals of someone who doesn't work well under pressure or who doesn't take stress management seriously enough.

Low Sales Initiative

Definition: Sales Initiative is the inclination of the salesperson to make contacts rather than excuses. Low Sales Initiative is the result of contact hesitation. Contact Hesitation is the collection of attitudes and habits that cause salespeople to place unnecessary limits on the number of contacts necessary to succeed. Reluctant to make calls, candidates with low Sales Initiative are likely to place certain types of people off-limits to prospecting or hesitate to use all available means for gaining entrance to new or existing business relationships.

How To Spot The Problem:

With SalesMAP™: A Sales Initiative score below 40 indicates the presence of contact hesitation. Check one or more of the six Contact Technologies (see below) to pinpoint specific areas of difficulty.

Without SalesMAP™: Sales Initiative problems are almost impossible to spot without the help of a validated sales assessment. In job interviews, candidates appear almost superhuman; nothing is too difficult or will stand in their way of succeeding. It's like fire walking at one of those motivational seminars; almost anyone can generate enough courage and bravado to scamper across the hot coals, once, to the cheers of comrades. The trouble with selling is that it is so every day and often so solitary. Refusals and rebuffs wear thin on many reps and they'll quickly develop excuses for avoiding the rejection.

One way to gauge Sales Initiative is to keep track of candidates who follow up their resume with a phone call or some other form of contact. Did your applicant phone ahead to confirm your interview? Did the candidate send you a thank you note or email after the first interview? These behaviors could indicate strong Sales Initiative.

Perhaps the best way to measure Sales Initiative is to build it into your interview process. If you can afford to be highly selective, only do second interviews with candidates who re-contact you. This may be the most reliable test for candidates with no previous sales experience. They are, after all, attempting to sell themselves to you as a recruiter. Applicants who sit and wait for the phone to ring are likely to exhibit the same behavior on your payroll.

Question: *"How did you generate new business in your last sales position?"*

Interpretation:
1. Is the candidate quick or slow to respond? Does the candidate's business generation model contradict or complement your own?
2. Were leads provided in the applicant's last sales job? If so, what attitudes toward prospecting did this practice create and reinforce? Salespeople with low Sales Initiative tend to view prospecting as unprofessional or as a necessary evil.
3. Watch body language and listen for any built-in excuses that are likely to inhibit productivity in your enterprise.

Question: *"What do you think are the major reasons that salespeople fail to close sales? Follow-up: Which of those reasons do you see as a problem for yourself and how would you handle those problems selling our products and services?"*

Interpretation:	1. Listen for out-of-balance Life Need themes in their answer. People with low Sales Initiative will be uncertain about how to solve the problems or will have unrealistic solutions.
	2. High Sales Initiative candidates will possess an eagerness to answer this question and will respond with action-oriented ideas about freeing up salespeople to sell. Experienced reps with high Sales Initiative tend to complain about the organization erecting barriers to contact initiation (too many meetings, too much paperwork, etc). Applicants with low Sales Initiative are more likely to make excuses for poor performance (high prices, poor marketing, out-of-touch managers, etc.).
	3. Watch body language and listen for sighs of resignation or any defensiveness.
Question:	*"How many sales appointments did you have daily or weekly?"*
Interpretation:	1. Another strong indicator of Sales Initiative in veteran salespeople would be their date book or appointment calendar. Candidates with low Sales Initiative are more likely not to have an appointment book. If they do possess one, many of its pages will be blank or contain only administrative appointments (meetings, paydays, etc).
	2. Watch body language and listen for excuses. Excuse-making is the hallmark of poor Sales Initiative.

Low Career Energy

Definition: Career Energy is the amount of physical stamina the candidate brings to a sales career. Selling is physically demanding, particularly for outside reps who work long hours and are often on the go. People who sell primarily on the phone should have above-average stamina, but not too much. Inside salespeople with high levels of Career Energy may grow restless in a sedentary position. Low Energy individuals start more tasks than they finish. Successful salespeople get proper rest and have a balanced lifestyle. They are energetic.

How To Spot The Problem:

With SalesMAP™: A Career Energy score below 40.

Without SalesMAP™: Career Energy can be difficult to spot in a typical employment interview. Candidates are usually well prepared and eager to make a positive impression. Energy issues don't generally show up until after the person experiences the daily grind of the job.

But there are some ways to spot Energy problems in the interview. Some obvious indicators of energy management issues include: Does the candidate seem listless? Do you catch the candidate suppressing yawns? Does the resume contain obvious typographical errors? If so, your candidate may suffer from low Career Energy. Fidgeting, finger tapping, and knee bouncing are signs of high Career Energy.

Hobbies are another indicator of energy level. People who relax with strenuous activity (jogging, biking, team sports) tend to possess higher levels of energy than individuals with passive hobbies (reading, movies, collecting things). People with high levels of Career Energy miss fewer days due to illness and are less likely to be overweight or visibly underweight.

Question: *"Tell me about a time in your career when you had to give it 110%. What was it and how did you specifically go beyond what was expected of you?"*

Interpretation:
1. Can the candidate provide an example?
2. What represents "110%" to the candidate? Is it enough for your company?
3. What was the event? Is it transferable to your business?
4. Watch body language and listen for excuses.

Question: *"Our most successful reps work long hours. It's not unusual to put in 60-70 hours per week. What's the typical work week where you worked before?"*

Interpretation:
1. Watch the candidate's expression when you mention the amount of long hours. Can you detect any element of surprise (you may have to be especially alert to small eye and mouth movements)? Does the candidate shift in his chair? These are indicators of stress.

2. Low Energy individuals often sigh when they talk about working long hours or express displeasure in other passive ways. High Energy individuals will not make a big deal of the issue, although some may forcefully attack the practice of their former employer as being unnecessary or a function of poor management. Don't be as distracted by what the candidate says concerning working long hours as how they say it. High Career Energy individuals are quick and direct. Low Career Energy reps are slower and indirect.

3. Without a history of heavy workloads, it's very likely this individual will not put in the hours required to succeed if you have determined that your top reps must work more than the typical 40 hour week.

Out of balance Approval Need_____

Definition: Top producers possess accurate empathy. They are sensitive to the give and take of relationships without becoming either overly agreeable or close-avoidant. This requires a balanced Approval Life Need; too little and a rep will be overly oppositional; too much and your candidate may be unnecessarily accommodating.

How To Spot The Problem:

With SalesMAP™: An Empathizing score below 30 (Oppositional, approval-avoidant behavior that doesn't care what others think) or above 70 (Empathizers who quickly accept client objections, are close reluctant, and are more likely to take the customer's side in an argument than the company's).

Without SalesMAP™: Empathizing behaviors are extremely difficult to spot, and are easily overlooked in the typical employment interview. Candidates are on their best behavior and tend to be more compliant than usual. Empathizers, however, never turn off the need for approval. On the other extreme, approval-avoidant individuals can be spotted using many of the same questions developed for out of balance control needs. Detecting the excessive approval drive of the Empathizers takes special skill.

One telltale behavior of Empathizers is they send many positive visual cues to you when you are speaking. For example, they are likely to nod their head yes in agreement with almost anything you say, even if it's something negative. Empathizers establish rapport quickly, which makes them very attractive to sales recruiters, especially if the company's sales process is built around consultative or relational approaches to selling. They are adept at telling you exactly what you want to hear. It takes a skilled and disciplined recruiter to spot someone who is too agreeable, too understanding, too nice; it is even more difficult to apply the unique behavioral interviewing skills necessary to uncover the approval-driven salesperson.

Question: *"What kind of manager do you prefer to work with?"*

Interpretation:
1. Listen for strong people themes such as teamwork or customer service. If your candidate mentions an appreciation for a manager who is appreciative and understanding, you may be listening to an Empathizer give expression to a need for approval.

2. One check for Empathizer tendencies is to not give any positive feedback as the rep speaks. Remain stone-faced. Full-blown Empathizers will sense your aloofness and begin adjusting their comments in an effort to gain your approval. Listen for apologies or shifts in logic or emphasis.

Question: *"What was your biggest pet peeve on your last job?"*

Interpretation:
1. Typically Empathizers initially deny any problems. They may appear almost naïve in their assessment of conflict or trouble.

2. If problems are denied, follow up by inviting the Empathizer to open up. Say something like, "Oh, come on. It's just you and me." Or, "I'm not going to tell anyone." One fault Empathizers have that undermine sales organizations (in addition to not being able to close sales), is that they are terrible gossips. If you put out the bait, the highly developed Empathizer will break down and make petty complaints, thereafter quickly reminding you that the issue is not important or will not be a problem in the future.

3. Watch body language and listen for a change in voice inflection that becomes whining or passively aggressive, followed almost immediately by an apologetic demeanor.

Question: *Ask the candidate to sell you your pen or pad of paper (anything on your desk). Shake your head no during the presentation. Give no positive feedback. Then, look at the candidate and say, "I'm not sure you have what it takes to be successful here."*

Interpretation:
1. Empathizers will back down easily when confronted with anything less than glowing approval. Does the candidate attempt to overcome your objection or does he give up? Could you afford this behavior if your customers and prospects raised objections? Salespeople with out of balance approval needs let the customer control the sales process. They are quick to accept objections and usually wait for the customer to tell them they are ready to buy.

2. Watch the body language for signs of undue stress or uncertainty. Listen for subtle shifts in the logic or direction of the sales presentation as the salesperson tries to intuit your likes and dislikes.

Out of balance Control Need_____

Definition: Selling requires persuasion and determination. Successful reps, therefore, must possess a balanced Control Life Need; too little and a rep will be overly deferential; too much and your candidate may be unnecessarily confrontational or oppositional.

How To Spot The Problem:

With SalesMAP™: A Controlling score below 30 (Deferring to the customer, may be hesitant to close sales) or above 70 (Commanders who over-control the sales process and are excessively competitive).

Without SalesMAP™: Commander behaviors are spotted with your eyes and ears. Visually, look at your candidate's face. An out of balance control need is frequently reflected in an inability to smile naturally. Commanders smirk. When you talk, their eyes focus intently on you and seldom move. This gives the appearance that they are careful listeners. They do listen well, but not for the sake of relating, but to gain a competitive advantage.

When they talk, Commanders speak in short, forceful bursts, punctuating their statements with finger stabs or by pounding fist into palm. Although it is more socially acceptable for men, women, too, may display assertive, dominant behaviors.

Question: *"What kind of manager do you prefer to work with?"*

Interpretation:
1. Listen for themes involving loyalty and respect. These are aspects of leadership critically important to Commanders. If your candidate mentions a preference for a manager who doesn't require a lot of teamwork or collaboration, you may be listening to a Commander, as people with high control needs prefer to work alone.

2. Watch body language for shrugs and other gestures that minimize the importance of the question. For the Commander, the best thing a manager can do is get out of his or her way.

Question:	*"What was your biggest pet peeve on your last job?"*
Interpretation:	1. Control-oriented individuals should be quick to respond to this question, as they can often be critical and fault-finding. Listen for a need to criticize those in power. Will the pet peeve likely resurface in your organization? How is this applicant likely to respond to your efforts to coach or manage?
	2. Take special notice of any themes that deal with difficulty accepting change. Commanders resist change and are likely to demand solutions to complex problems by returning to out-dated, traditional responses. They are notoriously suspicious of computers or anything else they don't thoroughly understand.
	3. Watch body language and listen for signals of someone who doesn't do well in situations that demand flexibility or change.
Question:	*Ask the candidate to sell you your pen or pad of paper (anything on your desk). Stop him after a few minutes and aggressively disagree with the approach or criticize him for something said.*
Interpretation:	3. How does the candidate respond to criticism? Would this response be appropriate with your clients? Salespeople with out of balance control needs may become belligerent and argumentative. If the control need is balanced, the individual should accept coaching and adapt the sales approach to the new selling situation.
	4. Watch the body language and listen for whining complaints or defensive criticism.

Low Goal Orientation

Definition: Goal Orientation measures the ability of the individual to set performance goals and work toward achieving them on a regular basis. Hire Performance is driven by objective data. Top performers know on any given day where they stand in relation to their goals – how many calls they need to make, how many appointments will yield opportunities to close sales that will meet and exceed quota. Poor performers are more likely to measure performance subjectively on the basis of feelings rather than by pre-planned, objective measures of success. High Goal Orientation reps will know where they are going in their career and will likely have a timetable for achieving their strategic objectives. Low Goal Orientation reps tend to watch things happen rather than make things happen.

How To Spot The Problem:

With SalesMAP™: A Goal Orientation score below 40.

Without SalesMAP™: Like Career Energy, Goal Orientation issues seldom manifest themselves in the typical employment interview. Candidates will be prepared for over-used hypothetical questions such as, "Where do you see yourself in five years?" Recruiters often mistake candidate enthusiasm for Goal Orientation. Emotional measures of performance undermine the motivating power of goals.

One simple behavioral measure of Goal Orientation is whether the candidate was on time for the interview. Strongly goal-oriented people will show up early. They come prepared with questions, particularly questions about the company's goals. Another window on the applicant's Goal Orientation is opened when you ask about performance standards at their last job. Did the rep have quotas? Were they enforced or, like some motivational poster, were they used for decoration purposes only? Can the candidate identify the success ratios necessary to meet performance measures? If not, Goal Orientation behaviors were probably not internalized because they weren't all that meaningful either to the company or to the candidate. In either case, it could indicate someone with emotional measures of success rather than a truly goal-oriented salesperson.

Question: *"What percentage of your sales calls result in presentations and sales?" Or "What was/is your close ratio?"*

Interpretation:
1. If the candidate has experience in sales, does the applicant know his or her close ratio?
2. How does this salesperson's experience fit with the ratios for your own product/service?
3. Watch body language and listen for feeling-oriented ways of measuring success rather than objective measurements.

Question: *"How do you know when you've done a good job?"*

Interpretation:
1. The more a candidate struggles with the answer to this question, the lower the Goal Orientation.
2. Listen for emotional measures vs. objective measures of success. Low Goal Orientation individuals use feelings to measure success while candidates with sufficient Goal Orientation refer to the number of sales made, percent of incremental sales, number of months above quota, dollars generated – number, numbers, numbers. Highly goal-oriented individuals with no previous sales experience should also measure success in the attainment of objectives rather than acquiring feelings.
3. This question will also quickly uncover selling style and unbalanced Life-Needs. The approval-driven Empathizer is likely to talk about getting positive feedback from the manager or others on the team (relationships). The attention-seeking Performers boast about prizes won and other forms of personal and professional recognition. The information-starved Analytical may go a little overboard on the numbers while the control-hungry Commander may discount the motivating power of anything and everything outside him or herself.

Low Goal Focus

Definition: Goal Focus is the ability to set and keep production priorities without becoming distracted by competing interests or goals. Goal Focus is a critical asset in direct sales, but can be a liability in situations that require salespeople to multi-task. Extremely Goal Focused individuals will be frustrated in organizations that flit back and forth between sales approaches or continually tinker with the sales process or product lines. The more multi-tasking is important to your sales efforts, the less critical Goal Focus may be to productivity.

Goal Focus is a problem for two types of people: 1) salespeople who are being stretched in many different directions from competing personal priorities, such as working single parents; and 2) individuals who may suffer from attention deficit disorder or who require more outside stimulation that most people.

How To Spot The Problem:

With SalesMAP™: A Goal Focus score below 40.

Without SalesMAP™: This productivity barrier is hard to spot in a discussion with a candidate because a job interview is special. Interviewees know the priority of doing well and paying attention to everything that is said. Focus problems typically don't show up until later, when the rep settles into the routine of the job and finds he has become quickly bored or distracted by outside interests. Low Goal Focus salespeople may be restless during the interview or have difficulty concentrating on the topic of discussion. Low Goal Focus individuals will frequently feel overwhelmed with their own busyness. Some acknowledge they have a problem setting priorities or saying no to the many worthwhile requests to their time and attention.

Question: *"What do you like to do in your spare time?"*

Interpretation:
1. Does the candidate joke or complain about not having any spare time? This is typical of Low Focus individuals. Follow-up by asking about some of the activities that keep the applicant busy.

2. If you hear a litany of interests and demands, do any pose conflicts with career? For example, a candidate dedicated to coaching little league may not work out selling life insurance or other consumer-type products that require extensive night and weekend work.

3. Watch the body language and listen for signals of someone who can't stand being bored.

Question:	*"Have you ever had so many things going at once that you unintentionally scheduled different activities at the same time? How did you handle that?"*
Interpretation:	1. Low Focus individuals do this often. With so many activities and interests competing for their energy, they lose perspective and become confused.
	2. Does the individual have a strategy for dealing with the need to over-commit, or does he allow himself to feel overwhelmed and victimized by his busyness?
	3. Don't confuse Low Goal Focus with being disorganized. Many people who are easily distracted have learned to cope with their Low Goal Focus by meticulous orderliness.
	4. Watch the body language and listen for signals of someone who is easily distracted.

Impaired Telephone Selling

Definition: Impaired Telephone Selling is the most expensive contact technology that impacts productivity in direct sales. Of course, it is the highest-ranking cause of failure for inside sales reps. If using the telephone to sell or set sales appointments isn't important to your marketing efforts, you can safely ignore this form of contact hesitation.

Impaired Telephone Selling is a productivity barrier characterized by discomfort with making prospecting telephone calls or using the phone for any sales-oriented calls. Individuals with impaired Telephone Selling skills would rather contact individuals face-to-face rather than use the phone and, in severe cases, develop what can only be described as a phone phobia. They have no difficulty using the telephone to make a doctors appointment or to order a pizza, but if asked to make prospecting phone calls, they hesitate and often show physical signs of stress (pacing, heart palpitations, etc).

How To Spot The Problem:

With SalesMAP™: A Telephone Selling score below 40 and Sales Initiative score below 50 indicates a current problem. A low Telephone Selling score and a Sales Initiative score above 60 means the individual has tendencies in the direction of avoiding the telephone, but those tendencies are not yet hindering the ability to initiate contact.

Without SalesMAP™: Contact technology issues can only be discovered in an interview by asking specific questions. For inside sales jobs, you could require the candidate to call you several times and conduct initial job interviews over the phone. Not only does this weed out the individuals who may hesitate to pick up the phone to promote themselves or your products or services, but it also allows you to hear how the prospective telesales agent comes across on the phone.

Ask the following questions only if using the telephone is important to promoting your product or service.

Question: *"Tell me about how you used the phone in your last job. How many sales telephone calls did you make a week? Did you prospect on the phone or use it in some other way?"*

Interpretation:
1. Does the aspiring salesperson react to this question in any emotional or stressful way? Listen to the priority given to phone prospecting in the candidate's experience. Follow up more assertively if the candidate was attracted to a previous sales job because appointments were pre-set by others.

2. Is the level of phone activity reported by the applicant acceptable? Will your contact activity mean a significant increase in phone activity?

3. Watch the body language and listen for excuses.

Question: *Bring up the subject of annoying telemarketing calls that we all get at home. Ask, "How do you handle those kinds of calls when you get them?"*

Interpretation:
1. If the interviewee invests a lot of emotion telling you how awful and intrusive these calls are, chances are good she doesn't want to be viewed by others in the same way. If a certain behavior goes against someone's image of himself or herself, the individual is not going to want to exhibit it.

2. A candidate who asks for information about your telemarketing approach is not necessarily suffering from impaired Telephone Selling skills. They may simply be comparing your approach to one they already know.

3. Watch the body language and listen for hesitation or other signs of discomfort or an inappropriate enthusiasm for using the phone. Some phone phobics overcompensate by lapsing into flights of fanciful positive thinking in hopes of throwing recruiters off the trail of their contact hesitation.

Out of balance Attention Need

Definition: Top producers are socially outgoing. They are comfortable striking up a conversation with just about anyone. They enjoy promoting themselves as well as the products or services they sell. These behaviors are driven by a balanced Attention Life Need; too little and a rep becomes shy and uncomfortable with promotion; too much and sales productivity becomes the victim of such vanity that the customer is reduced to a passive spectator. Unquenchable attention seekers act as if they know everybody and everything, but their sales numbers seldom show it.

This productivity barrier is more costly in strategic selling than in direct sales. Performers do poorly in any sales cycle that requires patience and problem solving skills. They are usually impatient with details and prefer an intuitive "just do it" approach to handling predicaments.

How To Spot The Problem:

With SalesMAP™: A Promoting score below 30 (attention-avoidant behavior that prefers to let others take the lead in social situations) or above 70 (chatty narcissists or back-slapping "good-ol' boys" who must be the center of everyone's attention).

Without SalesMAP™: Of the five Life Needs, Performer behaviors are the easiest to spot. Although most candidates show up to a job interview nicely dressed, Performers are in a special category of fashion savoir-faire. Their motto is "dress to impress." There's nothing wrong with a professional appearance, but for Performers, the clothes they wear, the kind of watch they own, the jewelry they flash, and the car they drive are extensions of themselves. They over-identify with the symbols of success. To the Performer, success is a "look," not necessarily rooted in performance.

They fancy hyphenated last names and initials in place of a first name. They put their pictures on resumes. The Performer's signature is a dead giveaway. They sign their names in huge scrawling letters with lots of flourishes, perhaps to the point of being illegible. Everything they do screams, "Look at me."

In addition to the visual packaging, Performers give themselves away by how they talk. They speak louder than most people and are likely to dominate conversations. It's not unusual after the first question for the recruiter to struggle to get a word in edgewise. Performers interview themselves.

Their laugh tends to be boisterous and unrestrained. Performers have a story or joke for almost any occasion. They delight in expressing these with broad gestures and dramatic voice inflections. They may affect an accent or have developed some unique pronunciation of a word or turn of phrase, all designed to grab attention.

Question:	*Compliment the candidate on his or her appearance or ask about one the obvious success symbols they've worn to the interview (watch, jewelry, fountain pen, etc.).*
Interpretation:	1. The more out of balance the attention need, the more the applicant will talk about the item; where it was purchased, the comments it prompts from admirers, where you can buy it, what it means, and much more. Notice the amount of personal identity invested in the object.
	2. As with Empathizers, you can gauge Performer tendencies by not giving any positive feedback as the applicant entertains you. Remain stone-faced. Pretenders will get rattled and become even more histrionic in their need to engage you. They may even joke about your denseness. Would this individual become a loose cannon if not given enough attention in your organization? Would the interviewee's ability to improvise be a plus or a minus in your sales presentation?
Question:	*"What are some skills where you need improvement as a salesperson?" Or, for someone with no sales experience, "What do you think would be your weaknesses if you were hired?"*
Interpretation:	1. Performers have a difficult time identifying any areas of improvement in themselves. They will either dismiss the question or answer it in a very superficial way. Does the candidate have any insight into his poor listening skills? Will your training be wasted on someone who is convinced he has achieved sales perfection?
	2. Watch body language for minute signs of stress as the Performer is forced to come to terms with being something less than perfect.
Question:	*Ask the candidate to sell you your pen or pad of paper (anything on your desk). Shake your head "no" during the presentation. Give no positive feedback. Then, look at the candidate and say, "I'm not sure you have what it takes to be successful here."*

Interpretation:
1. Performers are not even likely to hear what you said and may ask you to repeat yourself. They are experts at tuning out what they don't want to hear.
2. Performers will become defensive and not hesitate to argue with your assessment of their ability. Unlike more hostile Commanders, Performers are more likely to respond to your objection at first with a joke or an exaggerated expression of surprise or disappointment.
3. Watch the body language for clues that the candidate is feeling defensive; for example, pulling back, covering up, or facial expressions of skepticism. The Performer is frequently more interest in rescuing a bruised ego than interested in improving performance.

Out of balance Information Need

Definition: Salespeople must plan and organize their work, but not become overly compulsive or perfectionists. When the individual's Information Life Need is out of balance on the low end, his behavior is nearly identical to that of the Performer described above. When the Information Life Need is too strong, salespeople become bogged down in the paralysis of analysis. Peak performers do not allow the lack of information to deter them from making the contact and initiating the sale. Analyzers with excessive data dependency become perfectionists who unnecessarily slow down the sales cycle and bore customers with their endless questions or recitation of details.

Research in the area of salespeople's Life Needs reveals that this productivity barrier is the least costly of all five. One reason may be the increasingly technological sophistication of the sales profession today as compared to a generation ago. The information age requires that salespeople comprehend more complex global and market forces than ever before.

How To Spot The Problem:

With SalesMAP™: An Analyzing score below 30 (information-avoidant behavior similar to the Performer) or above 70 (overly organized workaholics in search of perfection).

Without SalesMAP™: Look for someone who is detailed and precise. A good source of clues will be The Analyzer's resume. Look for it to be both neat and filled with numbers and minutiae. Look at the candidate's signature. Analyzer's love of precision is reflected in a small and neat autograph. In the same way that they over-prepare for sales calls, Analyzers frequently come to the interview overly prepared. It's not unusual for them to bring a briefcase full of notes and reports. Don't be surprised if your analytical interviewee whips out a notepad or portable computer and begins taking notes as you describe the details of the position or talk about the company. Analyzers can't get enough information. They have a similar problem when asked to give information. They frequently drone on and on about all the details of an answer. One behavior common to many analytically oriented people is the tendency to look up and to the left or right they talk. This sign that they are thinking, searching for an answer, can become very annoying if it is persistent. Don't confuse the Analyzer's talkativeness with that of the Performer. The difference is in the emotional content. Out of balance information needs make Analyzer responses flat, expressionless, and more likely to focus on giving data rather than communicating feeling.

Question: *"Describe a typical day for me. How do you plan your work?"*

Interpretation:
1. Analyzers are likely to be list-makers and detailed planners. They typically have strong tendencies to be workaholics. They may cite work as their hobby. While this love of work may seem appealing to recruiters, it doesn't automatically imply higher productivity. In fact, the Analyzer's insatiable appetite for minutiae undermines sales productivity by slowing down the sales cycle and minimizing the number of contacts due to the Analyzer's emotional need to be absolutely prepared. Listen to what priority is given to client contact as opposed to getting ready to make the call. Does your candidate seem more interested in organization and tracking information than seeing people?
2. Watch body language and listen for monotonous recitation of details. Notice how long it may take for the candidate to formulate an answer. How would your clients and prospects react to this kind of presentation?

Question: *Ask the candidate to sell you your pen or pad of paper (anything on your desk).*

Interpretation:
1. Analyzers may ask for time to think through their plan. They are uncomfortable when asked to perform spontaneously. Would this response be an asset or liability in your sales environment?
2. Analyzers will focus almost exclusively on the features of the product they are selling and miss the emotional aspect of the sale. They are more likely to talk about what the product is or does rather than how it will benefit you, the customer.
3. Watch the body language and listen for signs of a need to collect, analyze, and recite the facts and figures or all possible options. Are you bored? How will your customers read this presentation?

Impaired Up-market Selling

Definition: Impaired Up-market Selling can be a very expensive barrier to successful sales performance if your product or service is marketed to high-income individuals or to the top officers within a company. Individuals with impaired Up-Market Selling skills put certain groups of people off-limits to their prospecting and business development efforts. In addition to income, some people are uncomfortable around those they consider more educated or culturally refined than themselves.

If your niche market does not include marketing to Up-market clientele, you may be able to safely ignore this form of contact hesitation.

How To Spot The Problem:

With SalesMAP™: An Up-Market Selling score below 50 and a Sales Initiative score below 50. (Remember to look at the Sales Initiative score when interpreting any contact technology area. The Sales Initiative number helps you know whether the hesitation is chronic or acute, actually hurting sales productivity or indicative of a potential problem.)

Without SalesMAP™: This and the remaining contact technology issues can only be discovered in an interview by asking questions specific to the behavior. Ask the following questions if Up-Market clientele are included in your target marketing.

Questions: *"What kind of people do you enjoy selling to and what kind of people do you not like selling to"?*

"What, if any, were the target markets of your last sales position?"

Interpretation:
1. Does the candidate put certain people off-limits to prospecting and selling?
2. Are the candidate's answers appropriate and acceptable?
3. Watch the body language and listen for excuses.

Impaired Referral Selling

Definition: Impaired Referral Selling lowers the productivity of salespeople who are uncomfortable asking prospects or existing customers for the names of referrals. They typically believe that asking for the names of friends and acquaintances could jeopardize the sale or embarrass clients. Empathizers frequently develop this impairment. They see lead generation as being unnecessarily assertive and prefer to have the customer volunteer referrals.

The problem is not a lack of training. Individuals with impaired Referral Selling know how to ask for referrals. The problem is emotional as they choke on the question when the time comes in the sales presentation to ask about others who might be interested in the product or service.

If your sales presentation requires salespeople to ask for referrals, you dare not overlook this critical skill impairment.

How To Spot The Problem:

With SalesMAP™: A Referral Selling score below 50 and a Sales Initiative score below 50.

Without SalesMAP™: Ask the following question if referrals are a necessary aspect of your new business generation strategy.

Questions: *"How many referrals were you expected to get from each sale in your last position, and how did you get those referrals?"*

Interpretation:
1. Does the applicant hesitate or raise questions about your request? Hesitation about the issue in your interview is a good indication the individual will also hesitate to ask for referrals in front of clients.
2. Watch the body language and listen for excuses.

Questions: *"Can you demonstrate for me how you ask for referrals?"*

Interpretation:
1. Does the candidate evidence any training in his or her technique? Does it sound apologetic or confident? Is the act of asking for the referral consistent with the rest of the candidate's self-presentation in the interview or does this behavior seem unnatural?
2. Watch the body language and listen for excuses.

Impaired Networking

Definition: Networking is the ability to mine one's personal sphere of influence for sales opportunities. In consumer sales, where almost everyone is a prospect, Networking requires that a salesperson be able to talk to friends and family about what he sells. In business-to-business sales, Networking may require the rep to use social occasions to establish business relationships. When this contact technology is impaired, the salesperson hesitates to mix business and friendship. The rep compartmentalizes his personal and professional lives.

If Networking skills are not important to your sales efforts, you may be able to ignore this contact technology.

How To Spot The Problem:

With SalesMAP™: A Networking score below 50 and a Sales Initiative score below 50.

Without SalesMAP™: Ask the following question if you expect your sales reps to network with others in their personal or professional sphere of influence.

Questions: *"Everybody has a circle of influence they bring with them to the job. Who do you know? Who's in your circle of influence?"*

Interpretation:
1. Does your aspiring salesperson hesitate to talk about the subject? Does he raise qualifying questions or apologize that he's not at liberty to respond with names? Does your candidate name friends and/or family members in his circle of influence?
2. Watch the body language and listen for horror stories about failed multi-level marketing schemes or other excuses to avoid opportunities to network.

Impaired Presentation Skills

Definition: Simply put, this is stage fright. If making sales presentations to groups of people is important to your marketing strategy, you need to uncover this productivity barrier.

How To Spot The Problem:

With SalesMAP™: A Presentation Skills score below 50 and a Sales Initiative score below 50.

Without SalesMAP™: Simple stage fright is relatively easy to discover. Straightforward questions are best.

Questions: *"Tell me about a time when you got up and made a presentation in front of a group of people. How did you prepare? What was the outcome?*

Interpretation:
1. Can the candidate identify such a situation? Does the subject admit to stage fright? What size group was it? This question may also help detect Analyzers and Performers. Analyzer answers should focus on the preparation and fear of looking foolish. Performers, on the other hand, see themselves at their best in front of a group of people. Their only stage fright is when the presentation is over and they have to leave the stage.
2. Watch the body language and listen for hesitation and excuses.

Impaired Canvassing Skills

Definition: Canvassing is the ability to comfortably make unannounced cold calls. This contact technology is most critical in door-to-door selling situations. Whether it's door knocking or expecting reps to drop by a prospect's place of business on the way to another appointment, Canvassing can contribute to your bottom line.

How To Spot The Problem:

With SalesMAP™: A Cavassing score below 50 and a Sales Initiative score below 50.

Without SalesMAP™: Behavioral interview questions are necessary to detect emotional hang-ups involving this type of contact technology.

Question:	*"Have you ever bought something from a door-to-door salesperson?"*
Interpretation:	1. Individuals with impaired Canvassing skills tend to see door-to-door sales as demeaning and unprofessional. They may perceive such selling as peddling and are less likely than most people to have purchased something from a door-to-door salesperson. Can the candidate identify such a situation? Do they relate the incident as normative or as an odd experiment?
	2. Watch the body language and listen for hesitation and excuses.
Questions:	*"Can you tell me about a time you just dropped by unannounced on somebody and tried to sell them something?"*
Interpretation:	1. Don't be misled by the words you hear. Can your applicant identify a situation? Does she flinch at the thought of "cold calling" or raise qualifying questions?
	2. Watch body language and listen for hesitation and excuses. Is it possible to succeed in your company without face-to-face cold calling?

These are only a few examples to get you started. As you gain proficiency in these skills, add your own behavior-based questions specific to your product, service or industry. Don't' forget what you read in previous chapters – individuals are often combinations of styles and may possess multiple barriers to productivity. You're looking for the most obvious behaviors—behaviors that give definite clues upon which you may build your hypotheses.

Watch the behaviors you see when certain subjects come up. Hesitation or discomfort with any of these issues does not automatically preclude someone from being a successful salesperson. These behaviors may, however, indicate delays or distractions in reaching optimum levels of sales productivity.

Third Interview (90 minutes to 2 hours)

In some cases you'll need to schedule a third interview for candidates. For example, you've narrowed your selection to two outstanding choices. Or, you may still have questions or concerns about whether a candidate is right for the job.

The third interview is a good time to pull in others on the management team. Introduce the candidate to her prospective manager. Watch how the manager and candidate interact. Is the chemistry right? Make others on the sales team available for a question-and-answer session or a social function. Later, get together and get feedback on strengths and challenges they may have picked up.

Another approach to the third interview is a "ride with." Ask the candidate to accompany you or another salesperson on a call. If you use this approach, be sure to give the candidate ample notice and provide a clear dress code (if necessary). You should also be prepared to provide some compensation if the ride with will take more than a couple of hours. Finally, you should ensure that your client understands why a second salesman is along for the ride.

What to do during the interview?

Here are the three priorities for you, the interviewer.

1. **Listen.** If you're not a good listener, brush up on your listening skills before beginning your interviews. Successful interviewing doesn't depend as much on asking the right questions as it does on listening to the answers you receive.

2. **Watch.** This goes along with learning to listen. Some call it active listening – being alert to visual cues, such as body language and fleeting facial expressions.

3. **Take few notes.** Note-taking can distract you from listening and cause you to miss important visual clues. It can also make candidates unnecessarily nervous and uncomfortable. Writing down everything someone says can be perceived as an inquisition rather than an interview. Note-taking can also telegraph clues to candidates about the kind of answers you want.

You know it's time to end the interview when ...

1. You find a major inconsistency in the candidate's employment history or self-presentation. Be suspicious when the candidate says, "Let me be honest with you." What was the applicant doing previously – lying through his teeth?

2. The candidate becomes frustrated, angry, or loses his temper with you.

3. The applicant starts to cry.

4. The candidate suffers from a bad case of "I strain"—every sentence begins and ends with "me," "my," and "mine."

5. The interviewee expresses overt hostility toward a previous employer or too quickly assumes a victim role in describing previous problems.

6. The candidate uses vulgar expressions, profanity, racial or religious epithets, or improper humor.

7. The applicant shows up to the interview dressed inappropriately.

8. The interviewee demonstrates a consistent pattern of interrupting you.

9. The aspirant manifests annoying habits. If they annoy you now, chances are they will annoy your customers, and your annoyance will only grow over time.

Conclusion

For employment interviews to be effective, managers need to prepare a systematic and objective approach. This chapter lays out a game plan for a multiple interview process, including how to review SalesMAP™ results with candidates. Behavioral interviewing is a technique that helps avoid asking illegal or hypothetical questions in favor of getting information that directly impacts sales productivity.

Chapter 14

Making the Offer

Now it's time to "close" the recruitment sale. Unlike the typical sale, recruiters don't initiate the close when they see a buying signal. During the course of the typical interview, candidates are likely to give you more buying signals than a blinking blue light special. Hire Performance demands recruiters know when the time is right to make the offer.

In this chapter we discuss two aspects of making the offer to your candidate:

1. Negotiating the package

2. Drawing up the contract

Negotiating the Package

Top salespeople don't stop selling their value to the company simply because they get the job offer. Strong sales initiative drives good reps to negotiate for better terms. Be more wary of salespeople who accept your first offer than those who push for more. This will be even more applicable if your type of selling involves negotiating price or terms. You may want to structure your first offer slightly worse than that for which you are willing to settle. Lower the commission rate or salary. If the candidate accepts it, you've saved some money and you know to begin your training with negotiation skills. If the candidate has the initiative to bargain, you'll have opportunity to evaluate his or her negotiating abilities. Either way, you can't lose.

Life Needs and Negotiation Style

Before looking at some do's and don'ts for professional negotiating, let's revisit your SalesMAP™ profile or your analysis of selling style. The same Life-Needs that guide perception and behavior during the sales process are also shaping preferences for the give-and-take of negotiation.

Here are some insights, drawn from research and experience, into how one's selling style might predict negotiation strengths and weaknesses and how you can use these to your advantage to recruit a winning sales team.

Commanders

Commanders approach negotiation as a war. For the Commander, it's not give-and-take so much as it is attack-and-withdraw. They perceive negotiation as the other side trying to take something away from them, and typically react by either becoming a bully or adopting a "take-it-or leave-it" attitude. The Commander's brain seems wired on a binary circuit – either it's all on or all off. If they don't attack, they ignore or minimize the importance of the people or issues involved.

Commanders don't negotiate. One Commander recruiter for a stock brokerage tells applicants who try to negotiate a better deal, "The last applicant that tried to negotiate terms just left and he was a lot more qualified than you."

Commanders sense the subtle but very real power shift as their role changes from interrogator (they like asking questions) to supplicant (asking the candidate to accept the job). They perceive this as being put at a bargaining disadvantage. They fear losing control. To counter these feelings, Commanders employ an interesting strategy: they preface the job offer with a litany of candidate deficiencies.

It sounds like this:

"Well, Bob, even though I'm not sure your background is what I'm looking for, and you don't bring near the client base of many I've interviewed, I'm willing to give you a try. But I'm probably cutting my own throat."

Minimizing the candidate's talent and potential helps the Commander feel superior and totally in control. They seldom realize this technique not only undermines teamwork, but plants seeds of future disloyalty and a need for retribution in the mentally aggressive candidate.

Commanders can improve their negotiating position by using their competitive listening skills and strategic decisiveness to quickly evaluate options and to make constructive contributions to the negotiation process. Effective Commander negotiators realize they can stay in control and get more of what they want by seeing the situation from both sides and suggesting alternatives for good decision making.

Performers

Performers can't, don't or won't admit to having weaknesses. They see themselves as good at everything they do, including negotiation. But Performers must manage two critical issues if they are to learn the art of the deal: 1) impulsiveness, and, 2) impatience.

Performers are convinced that they win people over to their side in any negotiation by their charm. Their need for attention blinds them to the relational subtleties and sensitivities required for good negotiation. For example, because they are concerned with how they look and sound, they don't listen well and consequently miss bargaining cues. They become agitated if they think they're not being taken seriously – a serious mental mistake at the negotiating table.

The Performer's impulsiveness violates a basic principle of good negotiation: be patient while the other side responds. One of my favorite tactics to trick a Performer into tipping his/her hand during negotiations is to start a sentence and then pause, as if looking for the right world. Invariably, Performers blurt out what they're thinking, finish your sentence for you, and totally compromise their negotiation position.

Performers can improve their negotiation skills by practicing ahead of time what will be done or said in given situations and then sticking with the script. Performers may need to consult with a Commander or Analytical team member prior to sitting down at the negotiating table. Performers function best when they engender good will in the negotiation, persuading opponents of their commitment to reach a professional and equitable solution.

Empathizers

High approval needs make it difficult for Empathizers to negotiate long or hard. The more accommodating their style, the quicker they are to accept initial offers. They may counter-offer, but usually only once to estimate the determination of their negotiating partner. One favorite coping tactic of Empathizers forced into negotiating situations is to temporarily go over to the other side. Empathizers tell others they personally understand and would really like to oblige, but the company or their boss or somebody else in a black hat has already made the decision. Empathizers play victim and cop out.

Empathizers contribute to the negotiation process with their strong listening skills and ability to sense the emotional tone of the conversation. Highly accommodating individuals work best in a supportive role rather than taking the lead in hammering out deals.

Analyzers

The patience and detail-orientation of Analyzers usually make them good negotiators. Because they intuitively remain emotionally aloof from the process, they gain the advantage of objectivity seldom discovered by Empathizers, Performers, or Commanders. However, this composure can also minimize their effectiveness as negotiators if they communicate an uncaring, cold detachment from the process. Analyzers are also less likely to get beyond facts and figures to find the personal motivations of people.

10 Tips for Negotiating a Pay Plan

Based on this analysis of style, here are ten key principles for negotiating the package.

1. **Never discuss specifics of pay until you're ready to offer the job.**
   You don't really know how much a candidate is worth until you complete your fact-finding. You don't need to shy away from compensation in early conversations, but if the candidate asks about the pay, respond, "Between X and Y, depending on skills and experience." Until you are in a position to better assess the candidate's skills and experience, you're not ready to talk money.

   NOTE: It is illegal to ask candidates what is the minimum acceptable wage at which they will accept the position. Besides being illegal, it's demeaning and petty.

2. **Don't forget the value of benefits and perks.**
   Benefits can comprise up to 40% of a pay plan. Don't overlook the value of insurance, stock options, bonuses, employee discounts, vacation, sick pay, company cars, club memberships, and other amenities. If a candidate lives nearby, that can also count as an indirect benefit, although you should not specifically mention it. If you can't budge on salary or commission, you may find some room to negotiate with benefits and perks.

3. **Always work for win-win outcomes.**
   If it's not a good deal for both you and the candidate, chances are excellent one of you will eventually bail out of the relationship feeling victimized. Constructing a pay plan that appeals to both sides calls for creativity more than cleverness. Avoid trying to beat up the other party.

4. **Stay professional and upbeat.**
   Never minimize or demean a candidate. Threats, ultimatums, and raised voices are indicators that you need to call a break in the negotiation process. Losing your cool gives the other side powerful ammunition that can be used against you, not only in the negotiation, but in possible litigation as well. Avoid getting personal. Keep discussion focused on the job or the opportunity. Avoid negativity. If you must introduce a negative comment, preface it with at least one compliment.

5. **Avoid unilateral concessions.**
   Don't give up anything without getting something in return. Likewise, don't ask the candidate to give up something without offering a matching concession. Negotiation is a two-way street. Building a winning sales team is impossible if teamwork is undermined at the start of the employment relationship.

6. **My price, your terms, or vice versa.**
   This is a basic principle of negotiation and a simple, practical way of implementing point number 5. If your candidate draws a line in the sand demanding a specific compensation package, you could stipulate the terms of performance. If you can't negotiate what you pay your salespeople, perhaps you can bend a little on how or when.

7. **Be willing to walk away.**
   If you can't say no, you're simply in no position to be bargaining in the first place.

8. **Mirror your candidate's style; avoid style clashes.**
   Knowing selling style provides valuable clues for improving your effectiveness as a negotiator. Your negotiation style must mirror or complement the style of the candidate.

   For example, your candidate responds to your offer by saying, "I need to check with (my wife, my family, some friends) before I decide." Mirror this Empathizer style by constructing benefits that appeal to the candidate's relational sensitivities.

   You'll remember that each style has a complementary style. For example, Commanders and Empathizers don't mesh well. Neither do Performers and Analyzers. So, in the case of the Empathizer, using a bottom-line, take it or leave it Commander negotiation tactic would probably prove counterproductive. Similarly, a Performer recruiter expecting a snap decision from an Analytical candidate may be unrealistic.

9. **When in doubt, ask.**
   Remember, you're inviting someone to join your team. When you negotiate, be careful not to bargain in ways that undermine teamwork by creating adversarial relationships. When you reach an impasse or stalemate, ask your candidate for help. Be honest. If you want the candidate on your team, but legitimately can't meet a compensation demand, turn it around. Ask the candidate to help you brainstorm some options for reaching both your goals

   Likewise, if you suspect that a candidate is using some negotiation trick or technique on you, just point it out. "Are you creating a false urgency by telling me you can go down the street?" Cleverness is no substitute for integrity in the negotiation process.

10. **Put it in writing.**
    The more complicated the negotiations, the more important it will be to commit your agreement to paper. Be careful not to confuse your "letter of agreement" with a job contract.

    The KISS theory applies here: Keep It Short & Simple. List whatever you've agreed upon, including compensation, benefits, job title, starting date, and terms of performance reviews. Include the letter as part of the employment contract.

Drawing Up the Contract

Ask your attorney to provide you with an employment contract that meets the legal requirements of your state or province. Typically, sales recruiters must address at least two legal issues in putting together the employment contract: non-compete agreements and work-for-hire agreements.

Non-Compete Agreements

Turnover is part of the landscape of business. Top salespeople have a way of being discovered by your competitors and moving on. Defectors can not only take your customers, they may also possess strategic information about new products, clients, and pricing strategies – information which could give your competition an unfair advantage. Many businesses attempt to control this risk by including non-compete agreements in their standard employee contract.

Non-compete agreements specify that if the salesperson leaves the company, she or he will not accept employment from a competitor or start one's own competitive business within a fixed limited time (usually 6 months to two years). Non-compete agreements must also specify a limited geographic area, usually a certain distance from the employer's place of business.

Non-compete agreements are illegal in some states and may be invalid or severely restricted in others. Your attorney will be able to advise you about regulations in your state.

Work for Hire Agreements

Work for hire agreements give the company legal ownership of all ideas and inventions the employee may generate in the course of doing the job.

For example, Gretchen sells widgets for XYZ Company. One day Gretchen gets an idea from a customer for improving the product. She discusses her idea with an engineer who was recently fired from XYZ. The engineer sees the profit potential, forms a partnership with Gretchen, and begins selling the new and improved Turbo-Widgets. XYZ sues Gretchen and the engineer under the work for hire clause of their employment contracts.

It's possible that if Gretchen and the engineer could prove they developed the product without any employer resources and that the new product is outside the realm of XYZ's business, the employer might have no legal recourse.

Again, consult with your attorney regarding the advisability and scope of any work for hire agreements that may be necessary in your employment contract.

Conclusion

Negotiation skills are essential for building a winning sales team. Knowing one's selling style can yield important insights into negotiation style as well as the bargaining tactics of candidates. The purpose of negotiation is to reach win-win outcomes for all parties. Be sure to consult your attorney for any legal issues involved in your job offer letter or employment contract.

Selling is first and always a people business. People come first. People can make doing business lousy or great.

Recruitment and hiring are human activities that can never be replaced with machines or tests because the most important thing about an individual (character, work ethic, integrity, motivation) can only be discerned by another human being who possesses these same attributes.

Therefore, our mission is to seek and select candidates on the basis of personal qualifications first and professional experience and skills second. Skills can be taught; character cannot. Experience comes easily. Integrity is the hard part.

Chapter 15

What We've Done For Others, We Can Do For You

For most companies and organizations, recruiting a winning sales team is absolutely, unequivocally mission critical. In fact, it can be argued that the quality of a company's sales effort is second in importance only to the quality of its product or service. Yet recruiting those top salespeople that winning sales team has for too long been a mostly hit-or-miss, hope-for-the-best exercise.

But identifying those candidates who can and should be sales super stars while weeding out the likely also-rans doesn't have to be left to chance or intuition. As this book has tried to make clear, recruiting successful salespeople can be reduced to a simple, straight-forward, time-tested system. It is a system that removes much of the frustration inherent in the recruiting process and, because it works, pays big dividends for everyone involved. It is based on two realities, both of which have to do with an understanding of human nature:

1. **Successful salespeople make lots of calls**
   Top salespeople all share one thing in common: they make lots of contacts. These successful sales performers may or may not be physically attractive, or unusually personable, or have the gift of gab. But they will understand that to make sales they must make contacts. Lots of contacts. Day-in and day-out.

   So it follows that savvy recruiters look for candidates who are likely to make lots of calls.

   It's as simple as that.

2. Those likely to make lots of calls can be identified

SalesMAP™ is a tool that identifies those candidates who not only fully understand that call volume is the key to success in most sales situations, but who will make the calls. This ability to consistently initiate and complete not just a few, but many calls has very little to do with personality. It has everything to do with each individual's sales core competency.

Just because someone performs well in an employment interview doesn't automatically mean they will make sales calls. Recruiters need tools to help them get at the truth behind the smiling face and energetic handshake of the friendly candidate. SalesMAP™ is a tool that identifies sales candidates' core competencies and does so consistently and reliably.

Successful recruiters, then, will look for candidates who, first and foremost, demonstrate initiative. They will set their own sales goals and pursue those objectives doggedly. The successful recruiter will also look for individuals with what is called a strong "sales identity." Candidates who fit this profile view selling as a noble and honorable career choice. Initiative and sales identity are found in every successful salesperson.

The best salespeople are also those with a balanced approach in their selling style. This means, for instance, that they can be flexible, with their sales approach tailored to each sales situation.

Candidates with these competencies – initiative, sales identity, balanced approach – have been proven to be those most likely to also make enough contacts (calls) to insure sales success. These are the people you want. SalesMAP™ can help you find them.

Companies and organizations are using the Hire Performance approach with dramatic results:
- A major provider of check services was experiencing a 70% turnover rate in its sales force. This was driving down not only sales, but team morale. Having tried a number of other training strategies, one courageous VP of sales started using SalesMAP™ to screen potential new hires. By hiring the right people, the company's retention improved by almost 40% in one year. And sales went up.

- A multi-billion dollar financial services company that found itself losing market share is changing its entire sales culture by using SalesMAP™ to screen out order-takers and replace them with reps who will not hesitate to make calls. In a single quarter, for instance, a regional office that had traditionally placed last in the country vaulted to first place.

- That same Fortune 500 company saw its percentage of new hires who met or exceeded quota increase by 165% in just two quarters (6 months). The only change the firm made in its recruiting model was the addition of SalesMAP™ and training its managers in how to use the Hire Performance system.

- One company determined that SalesMAP™ was literally worth its weight in gold. Every SalesMAP™ assessment they gave saved $9,056 in losses associated with making bad hires.

The Hire Performance system of recruiting winning salespeople has worked and is working for recruiters of all types. For organizations of every kind. And for companies of every size.

And best of all, Hire Performance can work … for you!